Blinded by the Sun
&
Sweet Panic

Blinded by the Sun revolves around a scientific fraud in an English University. Through the characters of three scientists, it explores how the pressure to succeed, and the need to create hype, can cause conflict within the modern scientific world.

In **Sweet Panic**, a child psychologist's understanding of contemporary life is brought into question when she finds herself stalked by the mother of one of her young clients. In a changing urban world, the two women are pitted against each other in a battle for the soul of the city.

Stephen Poliakoff, born in 1952, was appointed Writer in Residence at the National Theatre for 1976 and the same year won the Evening Standard's Most Promising Playwright award for *Hitting Town* and *City Sugar*. He has also won a BAFTA award for Best Single Play of 1980 for *Caught on a Train*, and the Evening Standard Best British award for *Close My Eyes* in 1[...] *Clever Soldiers* (1974), *The Ca[...]* (1975), *City Sugar* (1975), *H[...]* (1977), *Stronger than the Sun* ([...]) (1978), *American Days* (1979)[...] *arty* (1980), *Bloody Kids* (1980), *Caught on a Train* (1980), *Favourite Nights* (1981), *Soft Targets* (1982), *Runners* (1983), *Breaking the Silence* (1984), *Coming in to Land* (1987), *Hidden City* (1988), *She's Been Away* (1989), *Playing with Trains* (1989), *Close My Eyes* (1991), *Sienna Red* (1992) and *Century* (1994).

Stephen Poliakoff

Blinded by the Sun
&
Sweet Panic

Methuen Drama

Methuen Modern Plays

First published in Great Britain in 1996
by Methuen Drama
an imprint of Reed International Books Ltd
Michelin House, 81 Fulham Road, London SW3 6RB
and Auckland, Melbourne, Singapore and Toronto
and distributed in the United States of America
by Heinemann, a division of Reed Elsevier Inc.
361 Hanover Street, Portsmouth, New Hampshire
NH 03801 3959

Blinded by the Sun copyright © 1996 by Stephen Poliakoff
Sweet Panic first published in 1996 as a Methuen Fast Track
Playscript. Copyright © 1996 by Stephen Poliakoff

The author has asserted his moral rights

ISBN 0 413 70700 8

A CIP catalogue record for this book is available from the
British Library

Typeset by Wilmaset Ltd, Birkenhead, Wirral
Printed in Great Britain by Cox & Wyman Ltd, Reading,
Berkshire

Contents

Blinded by the Sun

Blinded by the Sun was first performed in the Cottesloe auditorium of the Royal National Theatre, London, on 28 August 1996. The cast was as follows:

Al	Douglas Hodge
Elinor	Frances de la Tour
Christopher	Duncan Bell
Joanna	Indra Ové
Professor	Graham Crowden
Ghislane	Orla Brady
Barbara	Hermione Norris
Charlie	Walter Sparrow

Directed by Ron Daniels
Designed by Tom Piper
Lighting by Rick Fisher
Sound by Simon Baker

The time is the present.

Act One

Scene One

The stage is framed by pale green walls. The paint has faded. There is a crumbling emblem on the back wall, dedicating the building to the Sciences, dating back to Edwardian times. The effect is of a once splendid, rather confident space, now decaying very slightly. Bench seats run along one side of the stage. A row of full-length old wooden lockers on the other. An old fashioned soft drinks machine, dating from the mid-sixties, sits in the corner, brash and incongruous.

Al *is facing out. He is forty years old, a beady, humorous, manner.*

Al   The first thing I ought to say is – I will try to tell this fairly. Although, clearly I will always have the last word. (*He moves.*) Luckily. (*He smiles.*) – But I will try – quite hard – not to paint too sympathetic a portrait of myself.

He moves casually round the stage.

This is pretty much, I think, how it happened.

He opens one of the lockers. It is full of transparent plastic bags, like scene-of-the-crime plastic bags.

And to help me remember, there are these. (*He surveys them.*) Maybe a slightly creepy way of keeping a diary, but surprisingly effective in bottling the past. They look a little disgusting I know, all bunched up, but individually they're fine, (*He smiles.*) and not nearly as odd as they seem.

He takes one out, stares at it for a second.

Inside, some of the objects that seemed important *at the time*, to help remember that particular day. Some very obvious . . . like this bag from around the middle of what happened – in it a faded colour supplement. (*He smiles.*) We made the cover!

He holds the unopened bag up to the light.

I'll open it when we get to it – but if I remember right, 'A science detective story, a tale of greed, deception, jealousy, and a touch of hate, in the unlikely setting of the chemistry department of a northern university.' A little sensational of course.

He throws it back into the locker, then turns.

Actually, it's even better than that!

He opens first the locker, takes out another bag and a jacket that is hanging there. He changes jackets.

So the first one I'm going to use is from the day I knew there was a good chance I was going to be terminated. (*He rips open the bag.*) A cinema ticket. I have no idea why that is here – sometimes one keeps the wrong things obviously, there is nothing to suggest Joanna here, for instance. But this is right – a handkerchief with a few specks of blood, and two perfectly preserved ginger biscuits.

Al *goes and sits on the bench seat, picks up cup of tea, and a tin of ginger biscuits.*

Christopher *enters, with mug of tea. He is the same age, tall, elegant, has an effortless charm and self-confidence.*

Christopher   You're still here.

Al (*grins*)   I haven't been in yet – but then I've only been waiting fifty-five minutes.

Christopher (*sits next to him*)   Oh, that's nothing. Anyway, if you'd been in quick that might have been ominous. Don't eat all the biscuits.

Al (*not giving up biscuits*)   Today I can gorge myself. (*Bantering tone.*) He'd never dare keep *you* waiting.

Christopher   I hope that's true.

Elinor *enters. She is in her fifties. Rather chic working clothes, formidable exterior, a mixture of old-fashioned teacher and something more mysterious, volatile.*

Elinor   I thought somebody had made off with the biscuits.

Al *deferentially hands* **Elinor** *the biscuits.*

Elinor (*peering into tin*) Just my usual. Have you dressed up for him, Albie, new shoes?

Al Yes – and that was a mistake. They're bloody painful.

Elinor He probably wants to see you about something very routine – don't worry.

Al *No.* (*He gets up.*) Bad news always comes on Wednesdays.

Christopher (*laughs*) Oh yeah?

Elinor According to whom, Albie?

Al (*nervous laugh*) No, I think it's true – people say 'I will do it by the weekend, fire the bastard!' But the weekend comes and they put it off – and then it's Monday, but they still haven't done it. Suddenly it's Wednesday, they have to act . . .

Elinor (*cutting him off, laughing*) Is this 'Albie's law'? Maybe it's going to pass into the language.

Christopher (*pleasantly*) It's bullshit. (*He gets up.*) Actually I have something in my room that you may enjoy – help distract you a little better than the biscuits.

He gives **Al** *a knowing look, which he doesn't see.*

I'll go and see if it's still there.

Al Thank you. Anything would help.

Christopher *exits.* **Al**, *alone with* **Elinor**, *glances over his shoulder.*

Al I thought I was being summoned.

Elinor Don't be so nervous. It'll be all right, Albie.

Al I don't think so.

Elinor (*she smiles*) They'd have to ask you to take extremely early retirement. And the last paper wasn't too bad, was it – it was (*Tiny pause.*) competent.

Al   What you mean the 'last paper'? I've only published two in seven years! (*He gets up.*) Would you keep me? (*Looking at her warmly.*) I mean – you never thought I'd last this long.

Elinor (*lightly*)   Oh, I don't know about that – you always had good excuses. The number of times I said 'Where's the work?' (*She laughs.*) You always had a super excuse.

Al   I wish I had one now. (*Very respectful.*) Have you got any advice?

Elinor (*taking a drag on cigarette*)   Just agree with everything he says. He's a vain old man. Flatter him, but not too obviously.

Al   You mean only do the first part on my knees.

Elinor   And not too many of your jokes either, Albie.

Al   You couldn't . . . (*He hesitates.*) you couldn't put in a word for me.

Elinor   I already have, two words – 'Albie's useful.' (*Warmly.*) No, I've done what I can. I talked to him.

Al (*quiet, grateful*)   Elinor, thank you.

Christopher *enters with* **Joanna***, who is in her early twenties. She has a local accent, and a very alert, watchful manner.*

Christopher   This is Joanna.

Joanna   Hi.

Al   *She* was in your room!

Christopher (*calmly*)   Joanna is a history graduate, and she's braved this department because she needs to check a few scientific facts for her Ph.D. (*To* **Joanna***, sharp smile.*) Dr Golfar will help you – he is *much* better at this kind of thing than I am.

Elinor   Maybe this is not exactly the moment, Albie.

Joanna   If this is not a good time.

Al (*looking straight at* **Joanna**)   No, this is a terrific time. Couldn't be better!

Christopher (*amused*)   Have to get on. Good luck, Al. I'll be back to see how the interview has gone. (*He exits.*)

Elinor   Goodness, I've got to get on too. (*She gets up.*) Just offer to tidy up his office, Albie, if all else fails. It'll be *fine*. (*She peers into biscuit tin.*) I think I'll take another one of these. Super. (*She exits.*)

Joanna (*imitating*)   'Super.'

Al (*watching her go*)   No – you should try to get some time with her. She's a very distinguished lady.

Joanna   Is she?

Al   Oh yes, she was closely involved in the discovery of the structure of vitamins, when she was very young. (*He smiles.*) She taught me. She's marvellous.

Joanna   What were all those knowing looks for?

Al (*innocent*)   Which looks? Oh – I'm about to be summoned into an important interview.

Joanna   Your friend seemed very sure you had a lot more time to spare than him.

Al   It's the truth. I do. (*Genuine.*) Christopher's very good, he's published a lot.

Joanna   And you?

Al   We'll come to me later! (*Pause. He smiles.*) Actually there's a very strong chance I'm about to be sacked.

Joanna (*very startled*)   What? Now?

Al   Yes. Any moment. (*Watching her.*) And *you* – it's very unusual to see a history student here. So what is your thesis on, Joanna?

Silence.

Joanna   The impact of the invention of detergent on public health.

Slight pause.

Al   That's a good idea!

Joanna You're kidding? Most people are usually speechless when I tell them.

Al No, no, it's good. History of how washing has changed – quite a sexy subject. Sanitation . . . poverty . . . whether people live or die. (*He smiles.*) What's more, there's very little competition.

Joanna That's why I chose it.

Al Precisely.

Pause.

Joanna (*looking straight at him*) Why did they think you'd automatically have time for me?

Al *hesitates.*

Joanna You usually have time for young female graduates, is that it?

Slight pause.

Al Always. Absolutely. (*Smiles.*) Is it that obvious?

Professor's voice Albert!

Al Here we go.

Joanna (*moving to exit*) It's OK, go on. The History of Detergent can wait . . . (*She exits.*)

Al *alone on the stage for a second.*

The large desk comes on, papers leaking out of its drawers. The **Professor** *enters, stands with his back to* **Al***. The* **Professor** *is a tall crisp man in his seventies.*

Silence.

Professor So what are we going to do with you, Albert?

Al (*quiet*) Oh shit.

Professor What did you say?

Al I said quite – that's a very reasonable question.

Professor Certain atmosphere of decay, wouldn't you agree, around the place? Even the buildings look disgusting, shabby. And this is a great department, with a distinguished history. (*He turns.*) I don't suppose you think of death very often, Albert?

Al   I . . . I try to keep it to a sensible minimum.

Professor   Did I tell you I was giving up this job?

Al (*watchful*)   No.

Professor   But it's not a surprise?

Al   Not . . . in so many words.

Professor   Don't be so mealy-mouthed, Albert, this is not the time. I'm seventy-two and feel older. I'm becoming Inactive Emeritus Professor. Wonderful title, isn't it. Inactive! Thank God. This will be in a few weeks.

Al   As soon as that.

Professor   Yes. Who do you think should succeed me?

Al   That's not an easy question.

Professor (*sharp*)   Isn't it?

Al (*exasperated*)   Well, maybe for you it is.

Professor   Now – and I want to feel you're being honest, Albert, how about Christopher?

Al   Christopher, certainly – that makes a lot of sense. (*Very slight pause.*) An obvious choice.

Professor   Yes, *but?* (*Impatient, very formidable.*) Come on Albert, tell me! (*Staring straight at him.*)

Al (*tentative*)   Well, the only question is, will he be off soon? He is working in a high profile area, at some stage he'll be tremendously in demand. Is this too small a pond for him?

Professor   Yes. And now – Elinor?

Al   Of course Elinor should get it – if she wants it. Her record is unchallengeable clearly, her great reputation.

Professor   But? (*Sharp.*) Come on, but?

Al   She's deep in her work of course. The only question is –
would she really like it? But if she –

Professor   I know all about Elinor, we go back a long
time.

Al   Then there's Hayward of course, Bogle, and Beattie . . .
even Warhurst. And we should advertise, we could go
outside . . .

Professor   Take too long. The situation is too urgent. (*He
moves.*) All the rest of the department are third raters. Dead
meat. (*He turns. Pause.*) I want you to do it, Albert.

Silence.

Al   What? (*Stunned.*) I don't think you can mean that.

Professor (*coldly*)   What did I say?

Al   I thought you said I should do it.

Professor   And why are you so surprised by that?

Al   Naturally I'm a little stunned. I'm not sure it's being
realistic.

Professor   Why?

Al   Because . . . because my reputation compared to the
others, my track record is a little thin.

Professor   Certainly there's no distinction there, a modest
record. In fact sometimes I seriously doubt you're a true
scientist at all.

Al   That's what I'm trying to say.

Professor   No, you're something much more valuable,
and much rarer – a born administrator.

Al (*startled*)   I've been doing a little admin for you, but . . .

Professor   It comes effortlessly to you. We've had buckets
full of distinction with me being here, and *look where it has got
us!* The department is profoundly unfashionable. It will
always exist of course, because of its history. But it needs
somebody who can reinvent it.

Al (*mumbling*) Don't do this . . . don't do it.

Professor What are you mumbling?

Al Maybe Elinor's expecting it. She should be offered first —

Professor (*cutting him off*) Elinor must be left alone to complete her latest research. And Christopher too. You yourself gave reasons why they shouldn't do it.

Al I didn't! I didn't mean I should get it instead!

Professor (*staring at* **Al**) The Vice-Chancellor agrees with me. And the Appointments Committee is also happy. I hope you're not going to refuse, Albert . . . I don't think that would be particularly wise.

Pause.

Al No, I'm not refusing.

Professor I told you, it wasn't a difficult question.

Al (*very quiet*) It's an honour. Thank you.

Professor Honour has nothing to do with it. The official announcement will be made tomorrow. That will be all, Albert.

Al Are you going to tell them? Elinor and Christopher. Explain it to them.

Professor (*surprised*) Me? Certainly not! *You* start doing everything, as from now. (*He exits.*)

Al *alone. He steps away from the desk.*

Al Oh, Jesus!

His head goes back, handkerchief up to his nose. **Joanna** *enters, slowly, she is eating chocolate.* **Al** *sees her after a second, out of the corner of his eye.*

You're still here!

Joanna So it appears.

Al (*smiles*) I didn't expect that.

Joanna   I just had to know what happened. Are *you* still here?

Al   It's not that simple. I can't tell you yet. (*His head goes back.*) Sometimes when things get complicated I get a nosebleed . . . it's just a few specks really.

Elinor and **Christopher** *enter.*

Christopher   You see, he's out already. I told you it wouldn't be long.

Al (*half turns*)   It didn't take long, no.

Elinor (*as she gets closer, sees the handkerchief*)   Blood! Oh, Albert – it's not that bad, is it?

Al   No, I'm OK. (*He faces* **Elinor** *and* **Christopher**.) At least for the moment.

Christopher   So what happened?

Al   Brownhill is leaving.

Christopher   At last! (*Buzzing with the news.*) I don't believe it!

Elinor   Good. That's good. We've been waiting for that.

Christopher   And he told Al first! When is he going?

Al   Almost immediately. (*He moves.*) Now, nobody say this is a joke – *don't* say you're joking of course. OK? (*He stops. Pause.*) But he's recommending . . . for some reason . . . God knows why, but . . . he's arranged to give his job – to *me*.

Silence.

Elinor   Albie – he didn't!

Christopher   Jesus. No.

Al   Yes! (*Self-mocking smile.*) Amazing, isn't it.

Christopher (*grins*)   For once you've really surprised me.

Al   *You're* surprised! I want to say right from the start, it's purely for administrative reasons. They want the true creative minds to be free, unencumbered, for their research.

(*Pause.*) Say something. (*Pause.*) At least it's the devil you know.

Silence.

Elinor (*crisply*) I think it's possibly a very sensible move. Good.

Christopher (*charming smile*) We'll have to make appointments to see *Al*. Form a queue, outside his door.

Al No, no, *no*. It won't be like that. Quite the reverse. We'll all plan together.

Elinor (*lightly*) Albie! Head of the Department! (*Pause.*) Don't worry, we understand. (*She moves up to him.*) There is no problem. (*She gives him a little kiss.*) You'll make a very satisfactory professor, I'm sure. (*She exits.*)

Christopher and **Al** *look at each other.*

Christopher Now the shock's worn off. Yes – Elinor's right. It could be very useful. (*He smiles.*) And it'll certainly be interesting. (*Pleasantly.*) You're much better suited to all that admin than I am.

He moves.

You see, you were wrong about Wednesdays.

Al I'm not so sure!

As **Christopher** *leaves, he indicates* **Joanna***, and says in a low voice.*

Christopher That was quick work, even by your standards, Al.

Al *alone on stage with* **Joanna***.*

Joanna Wow!

Al Wow, yes.

Joanna It's great, isn't it?

Al You don't understand. (*He pauses for a moment.*) I say this as a scientist, a realist, not out of false modesty I assure you, but because of the *facts*. (*He turns*.) Christopher is really good, a star, and Elinor, of course, is Elinor. And I'm . . .

Joanna   And you?

Al   And I'm pint-sized. A true hack.

Joanna   Are you? It's still fantastic. (*She laughs*.) Strange and fantastic.

Al (*smiles*)   It's a bloody nightmare.

Blackout.

Scene Two

Al alone on stage, takes jacket off, drapes it on chair. He closes the drawers of the desk. Peers at bag he has selected — then rips it open. Inside some coloured paper strips.

Al   And so now we come to these. They look quite innocent — like paper chains . . . but they were a considerable mistake. (*He exits with bag*.)

Joanna *enters, sits on edge of desk. She is barefoot, her clothes slightly askew, buttoning her blouse up, last few buttons.*

Barbara *enters, in her early twenties, abrasive manner, Lancashire accent. She stops very surprised to see* **Joanna** *sitting on desk.*

Barbara   Oh! I thought there was about to be a meeting. I must have made a mistake.

Joanna (*not completely concealing what she's been doing*)   No. There *is* a meeting. I was just leaving. (*Unabashed*.) Mr Golfar has been kind enough . . . to glance at some of my work. (*Slight smile*.) My research.

Barbara   *Professor* Golfar.

Joanna   Yes, of course, Professor Golfar.

Barbara   Easy mistake to make. (*Staring at* **Joanna**.) I'm sorry. I thought seeing somebody like you here, there *couldn't* be a meeting.

Joanna (*amused*)   Somebody like me.

Barbara   A visitor – from outside the department. (*She moves.*) I work with Dr Lathwell, and we've been asked to attend a meeting at precisely two o'clock. It is now 2.02. Elinor, Dr Brickman, has also been asked. They are both very busy people.

Joanna   Of course. (*Putting on her sneakers.*) I'll be as quick as I can I promise.

Pause. **Barbara** *watching her.*

Barbara   Amazing to think that in this room one of the first conversations about the creation of radar happened. (*Touching desk.*) *Right* here. And now –

Joanna   And now you've come right down in the world – you're stuck with Professor Golfar.

Barbara   Did I say that? (*Very sharp.*) I certainly didn't hear myself say that.

Joanna (*surprised by* **Barbara**'*s self-possession*)   No. You didn't.

Elinor *enters.*

Elinor   Oh, I thought there was a meeting.

Joanna (*putting on other shoe hurriedly*)   I was just explaining, I'm not here, I'm *really*, not here.

Christopher *enters, sees* **Joanna**.

Christopher (*breezily*)   That's a delightful surprise. There is no meeting – the meeting's been cancelled! I can get back.

Al *enters, holding cardboard charts under his arm.*

Al   No, no, no. There *is* a meeting. Joanna was just on the point of leaving.

Joanna (*laughs*)   Don't worry – I'm out of here! (*She stops by exit.*) Thank you for your time, Professor Golfar. It's been very useful.

Al   Absolutely. I'll await the next instalment with interest.

Joanna *exits. She has left her shoulder bag.*

Al   Joanna! (*He turns.*) I'll deal with that later.

Christopher *laughs at this.* **Al** *looks at him unabashed.*

Al   Her work's good.

Christopher (*amused*)   Of course, Al. It's great that you can find the time.

Al (*broad smile*)   Yes, I know, isn't it!

He looks across the room at them. The atmosphere suddenly more formal, as **Elinor**, **Christopher**, **Barbara**, *wait for him to speak.*

Please sit. Come on, everyone!

Elinor   We'll stand, I think. This won't take long, will it?

Al   No, no, of course not.

He is nervous, shuffling papers, for a moment not facing them directly.

You should see some of the things I've found in his desk!

Elinor   So why have you summoned us all here, Albie?

Al (*laughs*)   I haven't summoned you for Chrissake! This is an informal gathering.

Christopher   Why did you need to see us, Al?

Al   OK, OK, I would prefer this to be more relaxed, but still – (*Looking across at them.*) Jesus! This is not exactly easy for me. To address you . . . (*Pause.*) OK – I'm diving in *now*. You see these strips – (*Laying out coloured strips along desk.*)

Elinor   Strips!

Al   If you're red, Elinor, and Christopher's green . . .

Elinor   I'm a red paper strip?

Al   Yes, yes, just for today. And then we look here . . . (*Indicating chart.*) Over the last two years at the amount of *teaching* the red and green strips have done.

He holds up the big chart. There is very little sign of any red and green.

Elinor   I don't need to look at any chart to know that,
Albie.

Al   No. It's just with all due respect to Bogle, Beattie and
Warhurst, we have a priceless asset in the two of you,
Christopher, (*To* **Elinor**.) and you . . . you're star status,
your great reputation, Elinor. (*Swallows deeply*.) So, in order
to attract more students in the future, which we must do, I
want – I would very much like – you to teach more, to do
more bread-and-butter lectures. (*With chart*.) To have a little
more red here . . . and green there.

Silence.

Elinor   The answer is no, Albie.

Al (*with display*)   I just want to show –

Elinor (*calmly*)   The answer is no. I have always taught
once a week, for the last twenty-five years.

Christopher (*effortlessly*)   There are other priorities, Al –
the answer has to be *no*. (*Crisply*.) Is that it?

Silence.

Barbara   Can we go?

Al (*another deep breath*)   I was also considering – see what you
think of this – to help us with sponsorship from industry . . .
when we want to target a little of our research . . . renaming
the department, 'Energy Studies'. (*His voice tailing away*.) As
has happened elsewhere.

Silence.

Elinor   I don't like that very much, Albie, I have to
confess.

Al   No? (*He looks across at them*.) I'll keep thinking.

They begin to move. **Al** *coughs.*

And there's the room.

Elinor (*sharp*)   The room?

Al   I was just wondering, Elinor, if there was any chance, because we need to enlarge the computer room, of having a corner . . . a fragment of the space you occupy.

Silence.

Elinor   From my lab? No, Albie, that is not open to negotiation.

Al   Not open! (*Nervous smile.*) It was worth a try, wasn't it?

Elinor   I'm not sure it was, no.

Pause. **Al** *mock-strangles himself with the paper strips.*

Al   OK, I get the idea!

Christopher (*easily, as he goes*)   Al, I'm drawing up a list of other things I think you can help us with, OK? I'm sure you'll agree to them. Come on, Barbara.

Pleasantly to **Al**, *as he exits with* **Barbara**.

No more Energy Studies please.

Barbara   No!

Al (*to* **Elinor**)   Do *you* have to go?

Elinor *stops.*

Al   I made a mess of it, didn't I? (*He laughs.*) Don't know what possessed me to do a visual presentation – to you!

Elinor   There is no need to try so hard, Albie, there's not such a hurry.

Al (*very respectful*)   No. You're right, Elinor.

Elinor (*smiles*)   Of course I am. (*Indicating* **Joanna**'s *bag.*) You're still finding the opportunity to enjoy yourself I see.

Al   For the moment, yes.

Elinor   Does she know you're married?

Al (*amused*)   Elinor! I'm *not* married. Kathy and I – we're estranged.

Elinor   I thought you said you were working very hard on getting together again.

Al   Yes, we are. (*With* **Joanna***'s bag, poking around nosily.*)
Just occasionally that gets interrupted.

Elinor (*laughs*)   I see. Don't you dare go through her
things, Albie, really! Stop it!

Al (*reluctantly putting bag down*)   I can't be like Christopher,
beautiful lawyer wife . . . golden romantic couple . . .
faithful. (*Indicating* **Joanna***'s belongings.*) This is what I'm
like.

Elinor   Yes. (*Lightly.*) And not forgetting those odd plastic
bags you keep things in. Time to give those up too, isn't it.

Al   No, no, I can't!

Elinor (*lightly*)   You'll grow up sooner or later.

Al   Don't bank on it!

Pause. **Elinor** *moving.*

Elinor   There we are then. Super. (*She turns.*) I ought to tell
you, my work's reaching a *very* important stage.

Al (*very respectful*)   Of course, Elinor. (*Then casually.*) Is this
the work on mutant haemoglobin or is there something else,
entirely new, you are working on as well?

Elinor   That was a good try. When I'm ready, Albie.

Al (*smiles*)   You know going through the records I was
amazed to see how many invitations you get from all over the
world.

Elinor   You mean still.

Al   I didn't mean still! Would I ever say that? No!
(*Impressed.*) And you don't accept any of them.

Elinor   Well, they're easy to refuse – I find I don't like
flying any more.

Al   Really?

Elinor   Which is funny, because when I was young, I
always seemed to be flying places, often in rickety planes,
turning somersaults in thunderstorms.

She looks across at him.

So, Albie, you understand the situation – there must be no mention again, about changing my arrangements. At all.

Al   I promise, Elinor. An absolute promise. (*Sudden smile.*) There's one condition.

Elinor (*very formidable*)   Which is?

Al (*warm*)   You let me get you out of your lab for one evening.

Elinor (*startled laugh*)   No, no, I don't think so!

Al (*coaxing*)   Oh yes, just for once. Here you are, tucked away, living on the campus, shutting out all trivial distractions – when did you last even go into town?

Elinor (*joking*)   Quite recently! Sometime in the last five years I'm sure.

Al   We'll go with Christopher. All talk about work will be strictly forbidden.

Elinor   That sounds promising.

Al   We could celebrate your birthday.

Elinor (*lightly*)   I'm not sure I want to be reminded of my birthday. (*She moves.*) Well, if you can find something surprising, Albie . . .

Al   Surprising? (*Teasing smile.*) You mean, something crude and low down?

Elinor   I'm not sure about that! (*She moves, then turns. Breezily.*) And if I do come, I'm free of your interference for ever?

Al   Yes.

Elinor (*lightly, as she exits*)   You might just have a deal, Albie!

Al *alone on stage.*

The lights change. Shopping-mall muzak behind him. Neon light springs to life along the back wall. **Al** *is holding a third plastic bag—he opens it. He takes out a glass.*

Al One milkshake . . . the glass still stained with apricot flavour . . . a trifle caramelized now . . . a little lipstick visible on the straw. (*He smiles.*) This is our trip down town.

He moves, then turns.

An equation – possibly – begins to form.

Blackout.

Scene Three

The neon light. Muzak.

Al *is standing with a Virtual Reality headset on. He is next to the black metal Virtual Reality car with its joystick, but he is standing rather than sitting in it.* **Christopher**, **Joanna** *and* **Elinor** *are sitting on shopping-mall chairs.* **Christopher** *and* **Joanna** *both with milkshakes.* **Elinor** *rolling a thin cigarette. Behind them can be heard the intermittent sound of jackpots being paid out from the sound of the games in the amusement arcade. The sudden, heavy, pulsating noise of money pouring out.* **Al**'s *head flicks as he experiences the Virtual Reality images, the others watching him, calling out at him.*

Al Yes, yes . . . it's getting a little faster! (*Groping sideways for the joystick.*) Low, really *low*.

Christopher So what is it?

Joanna What are you seeing, Al?

Elinor (*calmly rolling cigarette*) Maybe we shouldn't ask.

Christopher (*grins*) Getting to the more explicit parts now are we?

Al No! No, hardly. (*His head moving.*)

Joanna This is a family shopping mall, after all!

Elinor (*smoking*) I hate the word 'mall'.

Al   No, no, I'm moving across a sort of idyllic landscape.
Just brushing the top of an English water meadow.

Christopher (*disbelief*)   Oh yeah?

Al   Now I'm skimming along a river . . . big fish, teeth
coming at me . . . girls sunbathing on the bank, dreamily
sucking a piece of grass, as I go by.

Christopher (*patronising, but affectionate*)   There we are, we
knew it.

Elinor   He's probably seeing something totally different!

Al (*taking headset off*)   Come here, Elinor, you must have a
turn, while it's still running.

Elinor   No, I can imagine it, Albie.

Al (*tempting, coaxing her*)   Come on, just for information.

Elinor (*getting up*)   OK, for you . . . just a peep.

Al *takes the headset, places it gently over* **Elinor***'s eyes.*

Christopher   Trust a group of scientists to be the *last*
people to try out Virtual Reality.

Al (*as he slips the headset on*)   And you have to give it at least
thirty seconds, OK?

Elinor *holding her head erect, headset on, not sitting in vehicle,
standing a little apart from it, the cable snaking behind her.*

Elinor   Oh my God, no, Albie! Really! You liar! You
cheat!

Christopher (*smiling*)   What is it? What have you done,
Al?

Joanna   What have you made her look at?

Elinor *alone, centre stage.*

Elinor   Jeepers creepers! It's flying, high speed flying. I
seem to be in the cockpit of something doing several
thousand miles an hour.

Al (*beams*)   It's called Flight Deck 2010.

Elinor (*moving with headset, groping for controls*)   At this precise moment . . . we seem to be heading straight for the side of a rather large mountain. (*She yanks stick.*) It's going to be close. Just pulled up in time! (*She laughs.*) This isn't very subtle, Albie! (*She moves to lift headset off.*) – shock therapy, for my fear of flying?

Al   No, no, wait! Don't take it off yet. Please – see where it takes you next!

Elinor *keeps it on, her head going back. Her figure tilts forward a little.*

Elinor   We're diving – Geronimo! Hurtling . . . right into the middle of a very tall building. Going to hit the glass –

Al (*laughing*)   It shatters!

Elinor   *Now*! Hold on everyone – we're roaring over the office furniture.

Al (*to* **Christopher**)   You should have a go.

Christopher (*charming smile*)   Don't need to. I've worn those before. I think it's strange how *crude* computer graphics still are, not remotely virtually real.

Al (*grins*)   It's not good enough for you. Of course!

He turns. **Elinor** *is standing, her headset at an odd angle, her body slowly descending.*

Elinor, what's happening?

No answer.

Christopher   Elinor, are you all right?

Elinor   What? (*Lifting her headset off.*) We were just going down a drain in the middle of the road in New York.

She smiles, leaving headset lying on stage, sound of money pouring out of arcade machines.

Thank you, Albie.

Joanna (*up to headset and putting it on*)   Is it still running?

Al   You wanted a surprise. It needed to be something you'd never normally do.

Sirens in distance, mingling with the muzak.

(*Taking headset.*)   What would you like to see if this machine could show you anything?

Elinor   *Anything*?

Al   Yes, you know . . . like, like . . . playing back your first sexual experience.

Elinor   Oh, I see! (*Immediately.*) I think that's quite an easy choice; it'd be wonderful to go into one's childhood and see exact reproductions of the landscapes and people one remembers, but do *different* things there, be good at everything one was bad at, have a Virtually Real ALTERNATIVE childhood.

Al   Yes, yes, that's a better idea!

Christopher *takes the headset calmly.*

Christopher   Or an even better idea –

Al (*quiet*)   Even better?

Christopher (*effortlessly*)   Yes. *Enter other people's past.* And be able to move around there without being spotted, seeing all the things they haven't been telling you, whom they really slept with, and when. How they *actually* behaved.

Elinor (*smiles to herself*)   That's nice, yes.

Al *trying to keep up with them, with their ideas.*

Al   Yes, it'd be tremendous to go into your past Elinor, be there as a witness!

Elinor (*surprised*)   Really? I don't think so.

Al   Oh yes, definitely. Seeing you when you were starting out, a young woman.

Elinor (*laughing*)   He's doing it again! I don't believe it. Reminding me of my age!

Sound of arcade machines, money pouring out.

Al   No, no, *no*. When you were working with the old monsters, doing your great work with Barker-Wyatt.

Christopher   Yes, *I* wouldn't mind being able to go back and watch you bossing them all around.

Al   This young girl (*He smiles at her.*) burning with conviction, with almost religious fervour, setting these older men such high standards!

Elinor   They always called me the 'female prodigy', like something out of Dickens! I can still feel their fat hands when I think about them – they used to give me these little taps on the shoulder –

Joanna   Did you go on picnics?

They look up. They've forgotten about her.

Elinor (*surprised*)   Picnics?

Joanna   Yes. (*Slight laugh.*) You know I always imagine boffins on picnics with their bicycles lying around in heaps, and you all playing cricket with hard-boiled eggs.

They look at each other.

Joanna   As you talk brilliant science.

Al *indicating clamour of burglar alarms in distance.*

Al   This is our version tonight. An urban picnic!

Elinor   Yes, you're right. We *did* have our picnics. They talked, and I sunbathed a few yards away.

Al (*suddenly loud*)   Oh, I'd love to have seen that. You on the grass, long hair stretched out, driving them mad!

Elinor (*lightly, smoking*)   I wasn't particularly successful at doing that, I promise you.

Al (*loud, intense*)   I really do wish I'd been there!

Pause. They look at him in surprise. The urban night sounds all around.

So . . . (*He moves, picking up headset.*) let's have another programme to see us on our way. (*He grins.*) How about, swimming with dolphins?

Christopher (*calmly*)   No, Al. I don't think I can stay here any longer. Burglar alarms! Amusement arcades! It's too depressing.

Al (*grins*)   I quite like it.

Christopher   Oh, come on, it's truly pathetic. Trying to imitate a corner of Piccadilly Circus – as if the original wasn't tacky enough. This town is never going to recover, it's like the university –

Al   I'm not *that* pessimistic.

Christopher (*smiles*)   Well, you're running the department, Al, you have to be a little more optimistic, and that's good.

Al (*grinning*)   Much prefer to be in America, would you?

Christopher (*lightly*)   I'm not sure . . . I certainly don't spend my time lusting after a lucrative position in the States –

Joanna (*suddenly*)   What if this could show you the future?

They look at her. She has picked up the Virtual Reality headset.

If you could put a coin in and it'd show you yourself in a few years' time, for five minutes . . . what would you see?

Christopher   Oh, that old chestnut –

Al   Yes, what will happen to us three?

Joanna   Oh, thanks!

Al   Four of course. (*Grins.*) I said four.

Joanna   Like hell you did!

Pause. The sound of the amusement arcade and burglar alarms.

Elinor   I'll be in exactly the same place no doubt, wearing the same clothes.

Al   That sounds right. I'll be bustling round the department, still trying to get its name changed.

Joanna (*laughs*)   I'll hope I'll be doing something original and provocative. *And* earning money! (*She turns.*) Christopher?

They look at him. Pause.

Christopher (*smiles, calmly*)   I'm not telling.

Al and **Joanna** *call out 'Come on!' 'Cheat!'*

Elinor   You mean you know! If you're not *telling*, you must know.

Slight pause.

Christopher (*calmly*)   I'd like not to be here. (*Smiles.*) But I probably will be.

Al (*grins*)   Aha. Something's brewing! (*He lifts headset, covers his eyes for a moment.*) No. Nothing's visible . . . the future cannot be glimpsed tonight.

Amiably, as he resets headset in Virtual Reality car, to **Elinor***.*

You know if you gave me the cupboard room, that little bit of your lab I need for the extension, we'd probably have room for one of these at work. Could nip in for a quick fix at tea-time!

Silence.

Elinor (*very steely, angry*)   I wish you hadn't said that Albie. Don't start talking about that now – *understand*.

Al   It was just a joke, I . . .

Elinor   No, it wasn't. (*Suddenly looking straight at him.*) So that's the point of this evening, is it?

Al   What you mean, the point?

Elinor   The *point* Albie. To get me relaxed, soften me up – isn't that the current expression, so you can start persuading me to give up some of my lab space. That's the true agenda of the evening.

Al   Of course it's not.

Elinor   I would take a very dim view indeed if that's what you were up to.

Christopher   I thought all those plans were dead, Al.

Al   Yes it was just a stupid remark, a bad joke.

Elinor   Yes it was. I will *not* have you interfering.

Al (*very flustered*)   I promised you, I wouldn't. OK. You've got to believe me. (*Moving.*) Shit! This is getting messy. One of those moments you want the ground to swallow you up. I don't want your birthday spoilt!

Elinor   Well, if you've forgotten your plans, I've forgotten what just happened. (*Icy.*) But that better be the case.

Al   Yes, of course. Come on, Joanna, we'll bring the car round. Give a moment for things to cool. (*As he leaves.*) Fuck! I want this to be such a good evening. Erase the last few minutes, *please*, they never happened.

He exits with **Joanna**. *Pause.*

Elinor   Dear Albie, he still needs house-training.

Christopher   He means well. He's just rather clumsy about it.

Elinor   I certainly hope he means well.

Christopher   Of course. This is *Al*, for Chrissake. What can he do to us? He worships you, you know.

Elinor (*startled*)   Worships? . . . No.

Christopher   Oh yes. He's in awe of you, Elinor. Of *course*. Always has been. He'll never cause us any problems. (*He smiles.*) What's more, it may cease to matter.

Elinor   Oh yes? (*She looks at him.*) That sounds nice and mysterious.

Christopher   Something I've been working on for quite a while . . . I'm not saying any more now. (*Charming smile.*) But just remember you heard it here first.

Elinor   Outside an amusement arcade – in a shopping 'mall'. (*She laughs.*) It is a repulsive word, I'm right.

She's pacing, smoking, her mood darkening.

I will *not* have him interfering in my arrangements, Christopher, under any circumstances.

Christopher   Forget about Al. (*Gently.*) Think how hard he has to run just to try to keep up, in any way at all.

Elinor *paces, then she laughs.*

Elinor   Yes, well, it's the last time he takes me out for a night on the town!

Blackout.

Scene Four

Al *alone on stage with next airtight bag.*

Al   I still wake up in a sweat sometimes thinking about that night! I did *not* take her out, to work on her at all.

He moves, stops, smiles.

Well, maybe ten per cent.

He peers close into bag.

So we come to what should be one of the most momentous bags of all. (*He opens it.*) But in fact there is only a half-empty tin of barley sugars, and a fragment of a child's picture. (*Staring at fragment.*) This was huge once.

Joanna *enters, scantily clad, summer clothes.*

Al   There were tiny hints that something was about to break . . .

Joanna *stands against the wall, he is up to her, kissing her shoulder, holding some papers in one hand, and* **Joanna** *in the other.* **Al** *turns back to us.*

Al   When it happened I was deep in paperwork, naturally.

He turns back to **Joanna**, *about to kiss her, then looks up.*

I wish I had been able to keep Barbara's sneakers – I will always connect that moment with her new incredibly clean sneakers!

Barbara *comes running on, wearing crisp wonderfully clean sneakers.*

Barbara   Have you heard?

Al (*moving a respectable distance from* **Joanna**)   Heard what?

Barbara   You haven't heard!

Al   No. What is it?

Barbara   I thought Christopher was coming here to tell you. You really haven't heard?

Al   No, we can do this all afternoon, if you like. (*Patiently.*) What is it?

Barbara (*excited*)   If you haven't heard, I don't think I can tell you yet. (*Slight pause.*) Afraid not! (*She exits.*)

Joanna   What on earth is going on?

Al   I think we are about to find out.

Barbara *reappears.*

Barbara   I've got to tell you! I can't stop myself, he's done it, he's made it work. (*Slight pause.*) He's done the Sun Battery!

Silence.

Al   No!

Barbara   He has. The Sun Battery!

Al   Jesus, I'm stunned. (*Momentary pause.*) I didn't know he was near something that big.

Barbara   Yes! I've got to get back, isn't it wonderful? (*She moves.*) He's almost ready to show you – you'll be called. (*She exits.*)

Joanna   That sounds promising, I like the name – The Sun Battery? How important is it?

Al (*slowly*)   We've got to remember everything about today. What the weather was like, what we're wearing.

Joanna (*startled, laughing*)   It's *that* important?

Al   Important? (*Exuberant.*) IT'S FUCKING INCREDIBLE . . . It's amazing. (*He moves, pacing, thinking.*) I knew he had an interest in the Sun Battery . . . but his main work is different. He must have been doing this on the side. (*He looks up.*) It's magnificent! (*He moves towards* **Joanna**.) Of course when you see it, *if* you see it, the enormity of it all will not be obvious. It'll just look like a tedious little tube.

Joanna (*excited laugh*)   A tedious tube!

Al   Yes – with minute bubbles. (*He laughs, he moves.*) You see, Joanna, you visit a sleepy science department, with all those funny smells you haven't known since school, and look what happens! You witness this!

Joanna (*loud*)   Al! For Chrissake, Al! Explain it to me. In words of not more than one syllable. Make me understand.

Slight pause.

Al   It's easy to keep it simple – Fossil Fuel is going to run out, right?

Joanna (*laughs*)   I can understand *that*.

Al   There is an almost unlimited supply of water –

Joanna   I can understand that too!

Al   Water contains hydrogen. But how to get it out? Some chemical reactions are caused by shining a light. Find the right chemical to act as a catalyst – shine a light, a beam, above all the sun – and you can create hydrogen out of sunlight and water. Hydrogen, which will run planes, cars, anything you want. And when you burn it, it will turn back to water. Polluting nothing. People have been trying to do it for years.

Silence.

Joanna (*excited laugh*)   I'll remember what I'm wearing!

Muzak. The equipment is brought on, supervised by **Barbara**. *A simple wooden table, completely bare, except for a metal stand and clamp holding a glass tube. The muzak really wells up. It is coming from elsewhere in the building, a radio blaring out light orchestral music. A beam of light stabs across the darkened stage. The tube starts bubbling.* **Al**, **Elinor**, **Joanna**, **Christopher** *stand waiting.* **Barbara** *a little apart.*

Al   This music is so inappropriate. It is the cleaners in the passage. Shall I . . .

Christopher (*gently cutting him off*)   Don't worry about the music, Al.

Out of respect, **Al** *lets* **Elinor** *move forward first.* **Elinor** *approaches the table, she stands alone in the beam of light, staring down at the apparatus. She takes out a tin of barley sugars from her pocket, all the time staring. She slips a barley sugar into her mouth.*

Christopher   Elinor? Do you see it?

Elinor   Oh yes. Absolutely . . . this is good. (*Very respectful.*) Is it based on titanium dioxide? No, no, I know nothing can be declared until the patent is through; the catalyst. (*Musing to herself, quietly excited.*) Is it anatase or rutile? You haven't used an adsorbed dye to shift the Lambda-max, clearly –

Christopher   The particles have an electrodeposited coating. It's only a few nanometres thick so refractive-index matching makes it –

Elinor   Yes, it certainly seems to have a high quantum yield. Maybe there's an added sulfonated surfactant to enhance mass transport at the surface?

Christopher   No. (*Warm smile.*) Think more a photocatalytic system –

Joanna (*excited smile*)   I can't understand any of that! But I saw the light hit the water and it made it happen. It's great to be one of the first in the world to see it. I'm getting goosebumps.

Al (*quiet*)   It does work, Christopher . . . it's beautiful.

Elinor *suddenly moves over to* **Christopher** *and gives him a little kiss.*

Elinor   Well done. (*Very crisp.*) I didn't think this would happen in my lifetime. Thank you for showing it to me. (*Pause.*) Super. (*She exits.*)

Barbara (*sharp*)   Is that all? Doesn't she want to see it again?

Christopher   She's pleased. That is Elinor being over the moon.

Al   I know it's an obvious thing to say but I'm going to say it – I'm proud to be here!

Christopher   I thought for one moment you were lost for words.

Barbara (*to* **Al**)   Do *you* want to see any more?

Al   No. (*Suddenly.*) I want to be alone with Christopher, now. Please, quickly. If you could . . . sorry to bundle you out – we must be *alone*.

The lights switch back on. **Christopher** *and* **Al** *alone on stage.*

You bastard! You've done it!

Christopher   Yes.

Al   It's fantastic news.

Christopher   That's right.

Al   I think I always knew! – I knew you'd do something big. And Elinor – just now . . . watching it, so still, but so excited . . . (*He is pacing.*) I heard on the grapevine Utah were making progress . . . but four years away probably, at least.

Christopher   I heard that.

Al Imagine what they'll feel like when they know! (*Gleeful.*) It's fucking great! (*He turns.*) Is the catalyst coated rutile? (*Laughs.*) Just a guess. What is it?

Christopher (*calmly*)   Not yet, Al. Not till the patent's through.

Al   Not even me? (*Quick glance.*) OK! I don't need to know till the right time. (*Excited walk.*) Let us compute what it means – the department is secure, obviously! *For the rest of time*. Millions will be coming in here. (*He grins.*) Millions for you too, of course. The Nobel Prize, naturally.

Christopher (*calm*)   Come on, Al, it may not be that big. It's got to be proved to be economic –

Al   I'm allowed to do this today of all days! That's what I'm here for. (*He looks across at* **Christopher**.) What a feeling it must be knowing you're getting nearer and nearer to something all the time – and only you and your research team know anything about it. What does that really feel like?

Christopher (*grins*)   Oh, Al!

Al   Don't say it.

Christopher   What was I going to say?

Al   That I think like a tabloid.

Christopher   But you do. (*Affectionate smile.*) And that's what's great about you. You're right, I'll have to know how I'm going to answer *that* question.

Al   When are you going to publish?

Christopher   I'm going to make a straight announcement first.

Al *turns.*

Christopher   That we've achieved it.

Al *very startled. Silence.*

Al   What? *Before* you've published?

Christopher   Yes.

Al (*urgent*)   Is that wise?

Christopher (*calmly*)   Of course. Otherwise it'll leak out. I'll invite Briskin and Moiseiwitsch over from Oxford, to inspect it, as a precaution. And then I will announce it immediately to the world press. (*Looking straight at* **Al**.) *When the patent is through, I will publish.*

Al   Christopher . . . don't you think you should wait till then? And let others repeat the experiment?

Christopher   What is this, Al? I've done it, for Chrissake. Why the caution? I *owe* it to the university, to show we're first.

Silence.

Al   What do I know? I'm sorry.

Christopher *moving.*

Christopher   You've helped, you know, Al.

Al (*lightly*)   Now that's a lie, quite clearly.

Christopher (*benign*)   No, you've helped – by just being there.

Christopher *exits.* **Al** *by himself. The apparatus is moved off. The lighting turns to strong sunlight.*

Al   So now we come to the child's picture.

He moves over to the bench seats, where a rolled-up picture is lying. Above the bench, is an old tannoy on the wall. He switches it on. A buzz of expectant chattering voices comes out of it, gradually building louder and louder, pouring out towards **Al**. *The sound of people waiting for a press conference. As* **Al** *listens, the service area of a cafeteria comes on.* **Charlie**, *a man in his late fifties, standing behind metal service units. One table with upturned chairs on it, placed other side of stage.*

Al (*listening to voices*)   The hacks gather, Charlie . . . even the weather is in sympathy. This terrific heatwave.

Charlie   Wonderful day, sir. In every sense.

Christopher's *voice, popping the microphone.*

Christopher's voice   'Gentlemen, gentlemen, please, I think we are just about ready to begin. I will read the statement and then you can ask questions. I have an announcement to make − '

Al *reaches up and switches tannoy off. Silence. His manner very preoccupied.*

Charlie   You're not going in there?

Al   Not yet, no.

Charlie   Prefer to keep out of the way, sir? Listen to it among the mushy peas?

Al   I *am* going to go in there and listen − in a moment.

Charlie   It's one of the best times I can remember in the thirty-five years I've been here. The old sense of excitement is back. And didn't we need it! People look happier, even when eating this food!

Pause.

Al (*quiet*)   We did need it, yes, Charlie.

Charlie   There's a real sense of going forward again, isn't there, sir. I could always tell when something was up with the scientists in the old days, because they'd come rushing in here with absolute ferocious appetites, just a few *seconds* before we closed.

Al *moving in thought.*

Charlie   I've seen all the greats we've had here, sir, and as soon as I got to know Dr Christopher, I knew he was − most likely − one of them.

Al (*quiet*)   Those have been my feelings, too, Charlie. (*He looks up.*) Sorry − you want to listen? (*Suddenly.*) Why don't *you* go in there, it's OK. Go on, I'll guard the cafeteria.

Charlie   Can I, sir? Good. It is something not to be missed, isn't it! (*He exits.*)

Al *moves round the cafeteria, preoccupied.* **Ghislane** *enters, a striking-looking woman, beautifully dressed.*

Al   Ghislane! What are you doing? Why aren't you in there?

Ghislane (*excited smile*)   Just came out for a breath of fresh air. The journalists are sweating so much! (*She looks across.*) Why are *you* here?

Al   Press conferences make me nervous. Not that I've ever been to one before. (*He smiles.*) This one is making me nervous.

Ghislane (*laughs*)   Me too! Do you think Christopher's doing it right? Is he talking too fast? Have you managed to hear any of it, Al?

Al   He's doing fine. (*He smiles.*) And you look fabulous, as always.

Ghislane (*warm, excited*)   Thank you, Al. *You* look just the same.

Al   You mean despite being a professor! (*Indicating the tannoy.*) Your whole life is changing in there . . .

Ghislane (*nervous laugh*)   No, no, don't say that!

Al (*pleasantly*)   Oh yes, you'll have to start practising law in America, because that's where you'll be. A big house! Celebrity! Christopher becoming a household name – as near as a scientist can come to one!

Ghislane   I don't want that for him. *Celebrity*. It's just good to know after all the incredible long hours he's done, it's all been worthwhile.

Al *watching her in the strong sunlight.*

Al   He need never do anything ever again, Ghislane, you realise.

Ghislane   Well, of course he will. He must. But to wake up every morning, knowing that you've achieved . . . whatever happens now! – You've done one of the most important things for . . . for goodness knows how long, by the time you're forty-one! (*Really excited.*) That must be amazing, knowing that, feeling that. (*She turns.*) It's bloody great, Al, isn't it!

Al Yes. (*Lightly.*) Not to mention the money, the books, the movie.

Ghislane *laughs*.

Al You can negotiate the rights yourself.

Ghislane (*laughing*) Stop it, Al, *please!* (*She moves.*) You've always thought that Chris had it in him, to do something special, haven't you?

Al (*thoughtfully*) Yes, I did.

Ghislane *doesn't notice his pensive mood*.

Ghislane So have I! (*Moving.*) And I've always loved him more than I can say. It seems the morning to say it. However obvious it might be! (*Indicating tannoy.*) Turn him up, Al, for Chrissake, I want to hear – we're missing it!

The volume up. Questions being fired at **Christopher**. '*Where were you born?*'

Christopher's voice A little unromantic village called Reddington in Shropshire.

'*How old are you?*'

Christopher's voice Getting personal. I'm thirty-eight years old.

Ghislane *starts slightly, glances round at* **Al**.

Al Really? So he's thirty-eight now.

Ghislane (*reaching up, turning the tannoy off*) A little embroidery! Very wicked. Oh, Christopher . . . ! (*She laughs.*) He doesn't want to reach forty.

Al Knocked three years off. If this goes on – he'll be twenty-five by tea-time.

Ghislane (*laughing it off*) I'm sure you've done it, Al! Doesn't everybody do it?

Al (*very slight pause*) Yes, of course.

Elinor *enters,* **Joanna** *just behind.* **Elinor**'s *mood is very up.*

Elinor So *this* is where you are.

Al We just popped out for a moment.

Elinor Yes. Well, the questions have got stupid now, it's time for a break. (*She laughs.*) Did you hear him lying about his age? The vanity of men! Really!

Joanna He did it very confidently too. (*Mimics.*) 'I'm *thirty-eight* years old.'

Elinor But he's handling it jolly well – I think they realise how important it is.

Al They must – even my seven-year-old daughter does! I've brought along a picture she's done, to show Christopher. It's on rather an epic scale.

He holds up picture. It shows a battery, like a colossal domestic torch battery, warming up the world, with the sun coming out of it.

This is the rain forest . . . and all the animals, being rescued by Christopher's non-polluting battery. Not very scientifically accurate – but you see it appeals even to the very young.

Elinor (*staring at the picture for a second*) Very striking, Albie! (*Teasingly.*) She's inherited your –

Al (*simultaneously*) My artistic talent. That's right!

Ghislane It's touching. You *must* show it to Christopher.

Elinor If he ever gets away from all the TV crews treading on each other. It's rather different from when –

Al (*quick*) You announced the discovery of the structure of vitamins.

Elinor Yes. (*Self-mocking laugh.*) But then of course we did it how it should be done – old George and I were photographed just for the *local paper*.

Al Didn't stop him trying to grab all the credit though . . . !

Elinor   Now, now . . .

Al (*grins*)   She despises anything commercial.

Elinor   Of course.

Ghislane   But a little hype is permissible – isn't it, Elinor?

Elinor   Today, yes, because it's justified. (*Moving across the cafeteria.*) No doubt soon, there will be science oscars – nominations for the best new treatment for stomach ulcers, or the best supporting Alternative Energy oscar.

Al   Why not? That's right! 'Best detector for explosives in an urban situation!' . . . (*Beginning to write in notebook.*)

Elinor   Oh, Albie, what are you doing? Not making notes today.

Al   Just one . . . 'The Science Oscars'.

Ghislane *has turned up the tannoy. The sound of people beginning to move as* **Christopher** *says 'Now, gentlemen, I would like you to accompany me to the laboratory.'*

Ghislane   They've finished. Great! It's all done.

Al   Yes – the story's about to go round the world. There's no going back now.

Ghislane   Al, stop it! He thinks our lives are changing for ever. (*Excited laugh.*) Well, *maybe they are!* And maybe that's good. (*She moves.*) Let's get in there! Come on, everybody.

Elinor   Yes, super. I'm coming. (*As she exits.*) You too, Albie, come on.

Al   Yes, I'm coming.

He watches her go, but he doesn't move.

Joanna   You've put your daughter's picture away. Why? I thought you were going to show it to Christopher . . .

Silence.

Al, what's troubling you?

Al   Who said anything was troubling me?

Joanna Don't play for time, what is it?

Pause.

Al I can't work out how he has done it.

Joanna So – is that such a surprise?

Al (*lightly*) You mean because it's *me* – that means nothing? That's probably right. (*More serious.*) But I've been reading what he's let me see. Even allowing for the fact he's keeping something back . . . it's (*He pauses.*) it's a little cloudy . . . (*He moves.*)

Joanna But you've seen it work. The demonstration – *you've seen it.*

Al Of course. I have, yes. So it must be true. (*Loud.*) I want Christopher to be right, for God's sake – I want this to be a wonderful day. I really do! (*Pause.*) It's only – I can't see how he's done it.

Silence.

Joanna (*whistles*) If it was a fake – Jesus! A *fraud* . . .

Al That is certainly not what has happened. That word must not be used.

Joanna It'd be amazing though, if it was happening – what a story.

Al No. *No, Joanna.* More information . . . I'm sure that's all it needs, to squeeze a little more information out of him, somehow.

Blackout.

Scene Five

Al, *centre stage. He takes off his jacket, moves forward in shirt-sleeves.*

Al Things become nocturnal now. (*He holds up fifth plastic bag.*) A tin of baking powder, Sainsbury's Baking Powder.

(*He stares at it for a moment with fascination.*) It would be fair to say this is one of the more important tins of my life.

He moves forward, pulls up the floor. The middle of the stage opens like a flower. A dark recess, like a large grave, is revealed.

As well as nocturnal, we get a little subterranean.

He climbs down into the recess. **Joanna** *enters, stands on the edge of the hole, staring down.* **Al** *is beginning to throw strange shaped objects out of the hole, fragments of broken scientific equipment, old jars of chemicals, both large and small, an extraordinary time warp of scientific detritus, many of the objects jagged and surreal. Music, some Bach, is drifting from somewhere deep in the building.*

Joanna   Careful!

Al *throws up another object, it spins across the floor towards her.*

Joanna   CAREFUL! Jesus, Al – what ARE THOSE?

Al   That's some tellurium bromide, from the early fifties, it looks like. Around the day I was born! . . . and here is some ferro-cyanide, even older, from the forties –

Joanna (*jumps out of the way*)   Cyanide! It's not leaking – not going to leak, Al?

Al   Don't worry. (*He grins.*) Just don't lick it.

Al *has come out of the hole, sitting on side, holding sinister and mangled piece of darkened metal.*

Joanna   And what is that horrible looking thing?

Al   This, believe it or not, is something very innocent, charming even.

Joanna   Charming?

Al (*stares at the fragment for a moment*)   Yes . . . You'll never guess what this once was . . . It is part of a very old computer terminal. Imagine how thrilled they were when this first worked. The joy . . . (*He holds it up to his ear like a sea shell.*) Can you hear the future?

Joanna (*takes it gently holds it up to her ear*)   Or the past . . .

Al (*he grins*)   People over the years whenever they finished with anything, they must have chucked it down here, didn't matter how dangerous. Just happily tossed it into this place.

He picks up another strange fragment, his tone more intense.

Amazing the merry incompetence that went on, isn't it! (*He stares down.*) When they were giddy with the possibilities of everything.

Pause.

Joanna   That's quite serious – for you, Al!

Al (*with another object*)   This is beautiful though – an ancient Kipps.

Joanna   Where's that music coming from?

Al   That's Elinor's music. She always has it on when she's working. If you can hear it, you know she's in her lab. (*He pulls out another metal object.*)

Joanna   That's really gross, Al, that one! I don't know what you're doing this sleuthing for anyway? What you expecting to find, that Christopher did something *here*?

Al   I'm not expecting to find anything. My doubts are almost certainly groundless . . . Just keeps me away from more admin!

Joanna   And what am I doing here?

Al (*unabashed smile*)   You just can't stop coming back for more.

Joanna   Really! (*Warm laugh.*) Patronising bastard!

Al (*touching her*)   You are quite properly intrigued by the situation . . .

He takes her arm, lifts her down into the dark recess.

Joanna   Not here, Al, for Chrissake, it's dangerous!

Al (*grins*)   Not while you're with me.

Joanna   You're sure? *Shit*! I'm touching something.

Al (*touching her breasts*)   That's some hexa-fluoro-iso-propanol.

Joanna (*her head going back*)   Hexa-fluoro-something . . . (*She laughs.*) I never expected to find old chemicals sexy!

Elinor *enters*.

Elinor   Albie! I might have known it was you.

Al *uncoils himself from around* **Joanna**.

Al   Elinor! Your music's playing – you should still be in your lab.

Elinor (*staring down at him in hole*)   I was taking a short break, when I heard some rather strange noises.

Al   Well, I was just – (*Indicating* **Joanna**.) well, you could see part of what I was just doing.

Elinor   Yes. And what was the other part?

Al   The other part? I, I, I was just checking there's nothing dangerous amongst all the junk that's been dumped here.

He produces another strange fragment of old equipment, out of floor. **Elinor** *is in a warm, exuberant mood*.

Elinor   The Professor of the Department needs to do that!

Al   Why not? I am a compulsive cleaner-upper. I used to ask to stay behind at school, so I could pick up the lost property.

Joanna   You would have!

Elinor (*lightly*)   I don't believe that's all you're doing here, Albie.

Al   Well, what do you think I'm doing? Keeping an eye on you? (*To* **Joanna**.) Elinor never goes home, or more accurately she's never *seen* to go home.

Elinor *is moving among the objects that are strewn across the stage, inspecting them*.

Elinor   Well, there are advantages to being single.

Joanna   A real obsessive scientist.

Elinor   I hope not! On the surface maybe. (*She laughs.*) I suppose I am usually either in the lab, or else stalking the passages.

Al (*suddenly daring to tease her*)   She passes by – humming Bach!

Elinor   Yes, well, I try to blot out all external noise with the music in my lab. Every now and then I stop it – and have a listen to the outside world, to check what's going on. (*She laughs.*) And I'm not missing much!

Al (*he grins*)   You're what Joanna thought all scientists were like – until she met me, that is.

Elinor (*straight at him*)   Yes, that must have been a shock – clearly Albie – meeting you.

She is moving across the debris, examining pieces with curiosity.

For some reason people still think of scientists as either evil geniuses who are totally oblivious to the effect of their work – good lord, this Kipps must be at least fifty years old – don't they? (*She picks up another object.*) Or else saintly boffins who are actually born wearing their white coats.

Joanna   And what category do you fit in?

Elinor   Do I *have* to be in a category?

Al   Ask her what work she's doing . . .

Joanna (*laughs*)   What work are you doing?

Elinor   Well, part of that is confidential.

Al (*loud*)   You see she's secretive as well!

Elinor   I'm only partly secretive!

Al   Makes all the difference. (*Teasing, warm.*) She doesn't have to dirty herself with raising sponsorship – has funding for life from the university. She needn't ever even whisper anything about her work, until *she* wants to.

Elinor   Yes – and it's wonderful.

Al *teasing tone, but suddenly very loud, more intense.*

Al Tell me what it is. The work. It's only us here. Come on, tell me, tell me now. TELL ME!

Elinor No, Albie. No, no, *no*.

Al Tell!

Elinor (*a great bellow*)   *NO*!!

They face each other.

That should be fairly clear – even to you, Albie.

Al *opening his mouth.*

Elinor And don't you dare try asking again!

Al She's so strict!

Silence.

Elinor When I'm ready, and not before. (*She smiles.*) You will be *among* the first to know.

Al Will I? (*Lightly.*) I'll try to be patient.

Al *opens a panel in the side of the stage, to reveal a cluster of more objects, spooky old canisters, large metal fragments, piles of yellowing papers stuffed into the skirting of the building.*

Elinor What have you found now? You'll produce a corpse next. (*She moves.*) Just think, with this breakthrough we will be able to rip all these passages out anyway! Rebuild – I might even get an extra room.

Al Of course. A whole new floor, Elinor – a wing if necessary.

Elinor (*warm laugh*)   Well, that might be a trifle excessive, Albie, a floor will do! Maybe a private bathroom . . . a Jacuzzi or two.

Al (*quickly*)   So you don't object to profiting from the commercial exploitation of Christopher's work then?

Elinor Don't be silly, I'm not *that* much of a puritan. (*She laughs.*) You think I'm daft! I will tuck into what we're going

to get, just like everyone else. (*She stops, stares across at them.*)
It's a splendid time.

Then she turns, more brisk again, moving to exit.

You'll put all this back, won't you. And a safety officer
should be called the very first thing in the morning. (*She
moves.*) And don't forget to switch off the lights. (*She exits.*)

Al (*watching her go*)   Yes, Elinor . . . (*Pause.*) I've never
dared to talk to her like that before . . . she was really happy
tonight, so I got away with it.

He moves.

Sometimes, she still treats me as if I'm nineteen . . .

Joanna   Sometimes I think you're in love with her.

Al *turns, smiles.*

Al   I admire her, certainly.

Joanna   More.

Al (*reflecting on this*)   You think? I'm fascinated by her, I
admit. The way she speaks, her 'supers', her barley sugars,
her arrogance, her scrupulousness, her ability . . . her smell
even.

Joanna   Her smell?

Al   *Yes* – you're transported straight back to the fifties. It's
almost as if she's bottled it . . . like the leather seats of a
classic car. It's addictive. (*He moves.*) I can remember those
smells from my childhood. (*He looks up.*) She wears scent in
the lab! It's wonderful . . . (*Staring in the direction of her music.*)
But she's still a real force, of course . . . still a great lady.
(*Pause.*) Soon we'll see the fruits of all that work . . .

*He starts putting the objects back into the hole. The more fragile glass
ones he replaces gently, the metal objects he kicks.*

Joanna (*keeping out of the way of flying metal objects*)   Mind!
(*She stares down into the hole.*) It's really strange to see among
all these old chemicals – a tin of baking powder.

Al   Baking powder? (*Louder.*) Where's the baking powder?

Joanna (*startled laugh. Mimics*)   'Where's the baking powder?' There! (*Pointing into the hole.*) And some bleach . . . What's the matter?

Al *leaps down into the hole.*

Al   Bleach! Oh shit, yes!

Joanna   What's the matter, Al? Why's that bad? Tell me – I hate not understanding.

Al *sits on the corner of the hole, with his tin of baking powder. Silence.*

Al   This will sound mad – but one of the ways of faking the Sun Battery . . . would be to use baking powder and bleach – with calcium hydride you could fake the whole thing.

Joanna   Oh, come on! Christopher used baking powder! You really can't be serious . . . can you?

Al (*quiet*)   I'm seldom serious, I know . . . (*Pause.*) But I don't like finding it.

Joanna   Distinguished scientists have seen the demonstration.

Al   Never means anything. They saw what they were shown. (*He moves.*) Conjurers always say the best audiences for magic tricks – the most gullible – are scientists. They believe what they see. (*He turns.*) He hasn't published yet, has he?

Joanna   But he can't have used something as simple as that. This is Christopher . . . ! It *can't* be that crude.

Al   Why not? Most notorious scientific frauds *have* been very crude. That's what's so interesting. They're sometimes startlingly blatant – people colouring mice for instance with black felt tip pens. Good scientists!

Pause. **Joanna** *among the debris.*

Joanna   But I mean, he wouldn't drop the evidence in here – *Preserving* it, for you to poke around and find. He'd destroy it.

Al   I'm not sure you're right about that. In a funny way this is where I'd put it too, among the other scientific equipment. That way you're not admitting anything, even to yourself.

Joanna   (*her tone serious, louder*) Al – you don't *really* believe he's faked it, do you?

Al (*loud, urgent*)   *I DON'T KNOW! I REALLY DON'T.*

Silence. He moves.

But any doubts are serious.

Pacing among the debris.

This is the one area of human activity where cheating still matters! It means your career is switched off.

Sharp flick of the fingers.

Just like that.

He stops pacing.

The thoughts are ridiculous – they must be – but they keep coming back . . .

He pushes the debris violently back into the hole.

Blackout.

Scene Six

Al *standing upstage by the lockers.*

Al   So where is it? The one with the deadly yellow notebook. (*Rips open sixth bag, stares inside.*) What on earth are these? Oh yes, a clump of ear-plugs, at least I think that's what they once were, they've changed colour. A truly repulsive exhibit I admit . . . but it's difficult to keep mementoes of lack of sleep.

Early morning light. The **Professor** *comes on. He stands next to* **Al**.

Professor   I thought I didn't have to come to meetings this early any more, it better be important, Albert.

Al   Well, in a way I really hope it isn't. *First*, I want to say about Christopher –

Professor   There is no need for a preamble – come to the point.

Al   Well, with respect I think I *do* need to say this. As you know I admire Christopher greatly – we both know how good he is.

Professor   A mistake. Never admire anyone.

Al   What? That's a very bleak attitude.

Professor   Of course. But they only disappoint. They *always* disappoint. I have never met anybody I've considered worthy of admiration – once I've got to know them. (*Suddenly turns.*) So, Albert, you think something's wrong with the Sun Battery?

Al (*startled, slight pause*)   Yes. Possibly. I think there is a *chance* the results are suspect.

Professor   He faked them?

Al   If you must.

Professor   What do you mean, if I must? What you're saying is – he's faked them.

Al   I MIGHT be saying that. Have you a view on the work? What do you think?

Professor   We are not here to discuss what I think, thank God. On the face of it, what he's shown me, is plausible –

Al (*relieved*)   Good! You're right of course. I should forget my doubts.

Professor   Did I say that?

Al   No, but I'm hoping you're saying that. I have no evidence, baking powder, his restlessness about being here, it's nothing! I have no desire at all to harm his reputation.

Professor   You shouldn't worry about that.

Al   Why ever not?

Professor   Because you have to protect the department.

Al   *I* have – just *me*?

Professor   A fraud would be *appalling* naturally. (*Pause.*)
But you can negotiate with him.

Al (*surprised*)   Negotiate? How do I do that?

Professor   Let him know you may have doubts. If they are
founded in any way, you can negotiate a retraction, 'the
result's no longer conclusive' et cetera, et cetera. But if you
are right, he *must* retract. You cannot just wait and see.

Al (*exasperated*)   I can't deal with this! He's a close friend –
what do I say to him? 'Excuse me, Chris, have you
perpetrated one of the biggest scientific frauds of the last fifty
years? . . . Oh really, you might have? Fine! Let's negotiate!'
(*Pause.*) And please don't tell me I'm Head of the
Department!

Professor   But you are, Albert. (*Smoothly.*) And in fact
news of your organizational skills have begun to spread
beyond these walls – how you've replanned the department,
stopped the rot here.

Al (*dismissive*)   Oh, really . . . (*He moves.*) I've just had a
brilliant idea, why don't you come back? Become an *active*
Emeritus?

Professor   That is clearly impossible. (*Pause.*) Does
anybody else know about this?

Al   No. Except Elinor. I sent her a short note, which I
rewrote many times.

Professor   It is not Elinor's responsibility.

Al   I know. But she is always a help to me.

Professor   She won't be. (*He looks at* **Al**.) It is a difficult
situation, Albert, I realise, but actually I think you're rather
better qualified to deal with it than most.

Al   Oh, really? In what way?

Professor   You have a curiosity about people, which I for one, completely lack.

Al *rolls his eyes.*

Professor   I cannot deal with their messiness, their contradictions, but I think you enjoy all that. And unlike me, you are not a jealous person. I'm afraid I have always been surprisingly jealous of my colleagues. Elinor . . . many others . . . (*He moves to exit.*) Since you ask my advice, Albert, I'll give you some. Hesitate and you might be finished, on the other hand, do something and you may prosper. (*He exits.*)

Al   Thanks! Great! (*Staring after him.*) Evil old sod!

The lights getting brighter, **Al** *sits at his large desk, sound of birdsong. In the distance people's radios.* **Al** *is on the phone.*

Hello, honey . . . yes it's me, Daddy . . . I missed my usual time to see you, I know. The first time ever isn't it, yes . . . but I've been up all night in my office . . . (*Lightly.*) Well, you know your dad – people leave him to arrange things . . . I'll be there next week, I promise . . . You've done another picture, of the Sun Battery? Is it as big as the other one? . . . BIGGER!

Barbara *comes bursting in, laden with baskets of food.*

Al   I'll see you, honey. (*He rings off, looking up.*) Barbara! Good lord, what's all that for?

Barbara   It's the picnic! You haven't forgotten, have you?

Al   The picnic? Oh no, no.

Barbara   We're all bringing things for it. Haven't you got something?

Al   Yes, yes, of course – somewhere. I think I brought a couple of tins of corned beef.

Barbara   You certainly splashed out, didn't you!

Al   Well – (*Mocking smile.*) since it's a time of celebration, I thought I would. (*He stares at her.*)

Barbara   You wanted to see me?

Al Yes.

Barbara Here I am then.

Their eyes meet.

Al Yes . . . (*Awkwardly.*) Have you been enjoying the last few weeks, Barbara?

Barbara Of course, it's been the most exciting time of my life.

Al Are you sure?

Barbara Am I sure? What do you mean by that?

Al (*moving rather groggily*) I know the tins of corned beef are somewhere – lack of sleep does funny things, forgive me. (*Casually.*) So you're not troubled by anything?

Barbara (*hard look*) What sort of things did you have in mind?

Al I think you know what I mean.

Barbara *looks at him blankly.*

Al Irregularities with the work?

Barbara No.

Al No? Just like that? (*Looks at her.*) No.

Barbara *No.*

Pause.

Al (*looking for tins*) I don't really think making a solemn appeal to your duty as a scientist will work with you, Barbara –

Barbara But you're going to do it anyway.

Al I'll just point out, you've been working very closely with Christopher. It's natural for you to blot things out, that you might have seen, that don't quite . . . fit. (*He looks at her.*) When you came running in to tell the news in your new sneakers, that morning, so excited! Was that tinged with anything? Any doubts? Were you thinking – if I shout it loud enough, it will make it true?

Barbara   We were *all* excited that day, I seem to remember.

Pause.

Al   Yes. (*Softly.*) You are very able, Barbara, I know that, ambitious, in a good way. If there is to be any unpleasantness –

Barbara (*sharply*)   Unpleasantness?

Al   There is no need for you to be involved. Your career could quite easily be unscathed if –

Barbara   That's not very subtle.

Al (*suddenly*)   I've never done this before – I don't know how to do it subtly! Jesus! – can one do this kind of thing subtly?

Barbara   And I've hardly got much of a career to scathe.

Al   You will have. (*Pause.*) So?

Very slight pause.

Barbara   There is nothing to tell.

Al (*loud, exasperated*)   I need to know the truth, Barbara – I don't care what it is, as long as I know!

Sound of **Christopher** *and* **Ghislane** *laughing, approaching.*

Barbara   You must ask Christopher. It is his work.

Al   Of course. Is that all, Barbara?

Barbara   Yes. (*Getting up.*) Yes. (*Moving her baskets of food.*) I have a little yellow notebook, with a rose on the front. It looks like a child's diary.

Al (*impatient*)   Yes.

Barbara   I made a few notes of my own. (*Slow.*) I'll go over those again, just in case. (*Pointed.*) I will reread them in the light of what you've said.

Christopher *and* **Ghislane** *enter, they are carrying baskets, groaning with food.*

Christopher   You don't look as if you're ready!

Ghislane   You *haven't* forgotten, Al, have you?

Al   No, no, no.

He stares at them as they put down the picnic baskets, his tone genuinely warm.

You look wonderful, you two. Great. As always.

Christopher   We thought we'd really overdo it, because we don't know when we'll all be doing this again.

Ghislane   We've got a lot of really strong cheeses, champagne, of course, smoked fish, smoked eel even. We could hardly move the bicycles!

Christopher   There's enough food here even for you, Al.

Ghislane   And hats! Of course! So we could really be like one of those vintage picnics.

Barbara   A boffins' picnic.

Al   Yes – I have a tin of spam somewhere. No, no, I malign myself, two tins of corned beef.

Christopher (*laughs*)   Al, we're honoured.

Al   Yes. (*Moving.*) I need to have a word with Christopher.

Christopher (*very elated*)   Fine. What is it?

Al   No, I need to make a time, an appointment with you.

Christopher   An appointment? That's very formal. It might be a little difficult, because we're going to the States first thing in the morning.

Al   What, so soon? For how long?

Ghislane   A couple of months. There's so much interest in him, he's going initially just for some exploratory talks.

Barbara *gathering bags.*

Barbara (*to* **Ghislane**)   I'll help you get these things into the car, while they talk. I can smell the cheeses, from here, they'll probably set alarms off, they're so strong.

Ghislane (*surprised*)   Right. OK. (*She laughs.*) If we must! (*Picking up bags.*) Don't you dare keep him long, Al, please!

They exit.

Al   They've forgotten the fruit. (*Staring after them.*) There's never any time now, is there?

Christopher (*breezily*)   There was never any time, with us, not really. Always been too busy. (*Looking at* **Al**.) What is it, Al?

Al (*deep breath*)   Being busy . . . that touches on what I wanted to say. (*He moves.*) Since you made your announcement to the press, everything has gone at such a speed —

Christopher (*smiling at this*)   Yes?

Al   You don't . . . you don't think anything could have been overlooked?

Christopher   What do you think I've overlooked, Al?

Al   I don't *think* you've overlooked anything, I just want to know if there's the slightest possibility that something might have been missed.

Christopher   You'll have to be more specific.

Slight pause.

Al (*swallowing*)   I mean . . . there aren't any inconsistencies . . . anything that could have been *fudged*?

Christopher   Fudged . . . ? (*Spontaneous laugh.*) You're not suggesting I've been cheating, Al?

Al *stranded centre stage.*

Al   I . . . no . . . I . . .

Christopher (*warm laugh*)   You are! Aren't you? Almost! (*He smiles relaxed.*) You little fucker.

Al   No, no, I just want to be sure. (*He looks straight at him.*) This little fucker just wants to be absolutely sure.

Christopher (*relaxed*)   You really think I would fudge results, risk everything, when it could be disproved in ten minutes. It makes no sense at all.

Al (*nervous laugh*)   You would have to be crazy, I know!

Christopher   What is this, Al? You don't want it to be happening?

Al   Of course I want it to be successful – more than anything.

Christopher (*softly*)   Yes. I think you do.

Al (*urgent*)   There just mustn't be any little kinks we don't know about.

Christopher   I promise you, Al – listen to this – everything is fine, everything has been achieved. *There are no kinks*.

Al (*quickly*)   Nothing Barbara or anybody else might have done for demonstration purposes . . . to help along just one demonstration.

Al *nervously pulls at bag of grapes.*

Christopher (*very firm*)   Al – there's absolutely nothing that can be produced to shake the results in any way. Nothing – not even in a plastic bag.

Silence.

Al   Right, of course, I'm sorry to have mentioned anything.

Christopher (*nonchalantly*)   No, no, you had to probe. You were doing your job. I understand.

Ghislane *and* **Barbara** *enter.*

Ghislane   Look at them, they've started eating the food! Al, you're eating the picnic.

Al   Am I? Oh yes.

Barbara   He forgot to bring his share – and now he's eating the rest!

Christopher (*grins*)   He's been interrogating me – that always makes people hungry.

Ghislane   Interrogating you, today . . . what on earth for?

Al   I just needed reassurance.

Barbara (*sharp, watchful*)   And did you get it?

Christopher   Yes. At least I hope he did. (*Fondly, looking at him.*) You mustn't worry, Al – these are great days.

Al   Yes, I know – great days.

Elinor *and* **Joanna** *enter all dressed up.*

Elinor   Are we late? I hope we're not late.

Joanna (*staring at* **Al***'s crumpled appearance*)   Looking at Al – I don't think we can be.

Al (*startled*)   Why's everybody dressed up? – It's only a picnic!

Elinor   But it's a celebration too – it's important to do these things properly.

Al (*private, close to her*)   Elinor, can I . . .

Elinor (*seemingly not hearing, indicating* **Christopher**)   It's the least he deserves!

Joanna (*to* **Al**)   And I hope it's the day you decide we are going on holiday together.

Al *tries to get* **Elinor***'s attention, he glances at* **Joanna**.

Al   You and me? Together? (*Slight pause.*) Of course. (*Direct, urgent.*) Elinor?

Sound from outside, people playing computer games in nearby rooms. **Elinor** *is standing with her back to* **Al**.

Christopher   Come on, everybody, let's get out of here before the weather changes! Barbara, have you got the camera, have you remembered?

Barbara   Oh yes, I'm going to be official photographer. There're going to be some great pictures −

Ghislane   Of this historic feast.

Barbara *exits.*

Elinor (*moving*)   I think I might even allow myself to catch some sun today. (*She laughs.*) My skin will have the shock of its life! Albie! Ready?

Al   Nearly . . . I'm still looking for my contribution.

Ghislane (*laughs*)   Oh, Al − you're incorrigible.

Christopher (*as they exit*)   I really don't think we need two tins of spam somehow, Al.

Al   Corned beef. I must find it.

Elinor, *on the other side of the stage,* **Al** *watching* **Ghislane** *leave.*

Al   She looks fabulous, doesn't she, Ghislane, really glowing, alive.

Elinor   Naturally, it's the happiest time of her life.

Al *and* **Elinor** *alone.* **Elinor** *not facing him.*

Al   Elinor . . . did you get my note?

Elinor (*she turns*)   Yes. (*Pause, quiet.*) It was one of the most shocking things I've ever read.

Al (*chastened*)   Is that what you think?

Elinor (*suddenly looking straight at him*)   How can you begin to conceive that he has done such a thing?

Al (*nervous*)   I don't know how I can either . . . but I'm beginning to feel fairly sure he has −

Elinor   Christopher! Who's already successful! What possible reason do you think he would have for doing something so idiotic? (*Very sharp.*) Why would he do that, Albie?

Al   I don't know. I DON'T KNOW. (*He moves.*) Fame perhaps.

Elinor   Rubbish, don't be so banal, *that* is truly banal.

Al   Well, people do strange things for celebrity now. You read about young artists killing themselves because they're not famous by the time they're thirty! Maybe Christopher wanted it so BADLY.

Elinor   Oh, come on, for goodness sake – you may find it possible to imagine that about Christopher, but I can't.

Al   Competition then – he heard somebody else was getting close.

Elinor   Nonsense, we both know at the moment there is no one else anywhere near the Sun Battery.

Al   We can't be sure about that, clearly! Or money – there's so much at stake, the *money* –

Elinor   Christopher's never been interested in money.

Al   With respect –

Elinor (*icy*)   Yes?

Al (*very nervous. Facing up to her*)   You don't go out much, you may not be aware of the pressures. The commercial pressures.

Elinor   I don't move around a lot, Albie, as you keep pointing out – but that doesn't mean I'm out of touch! (*Very sharp.*) And explain to me how Christopher planned to make money out of this, if it's a fake. (*She stares at him.*) That is just such sloppy thinking.

Al   I admit these explanations are too easy. But I'm working on it.

Elinor   I bet you are.

Al (*excited, loud*)   Well, something's happened! I *asked* him directly. I had to ask him just now. AND I DIDN'T BELIEVE HIM. (*He moves.*) And that makes things very difficult . . .

Elinor (*rolling a cigarette*)   Albie, calm down . . . please.

Pause. The sound of the computer games, an elongated burst from them.

Al   So what do I do, Elinor?

Elinor   Do? You do nothing.

Slight pause.

Al (*surprised*)   Nothing? But I think Barbara is going to talk to me about what has occurred. If I get evidence . . .

Elinor   You still do nothing.

The zigzagging sound of the computers. Then silence. **Al** *is truly startled.*

Al   Even if I get evidence

Elinor   I don't think that's remotely likely. And any evidence will be challengeable. (*Pause.*) But even then, yes.

Al (*amazed*)   What?

Elinor   Yes. (*Calmly rolling cigarette.*) If, and I don't believe there is an if, but if anything inexplicable has occurred, it has happened with us knowing Christopher is very very close . . . the notes he's let us see indicate there's definitely new work there.

Al *stares at her.*

Elinor   By the time he feels it right to publish it will be very clear how he's done it. And the people round the world who are waiting right now to reproduce the experiment, will be able to do so and applaud his achievement.

Silence.

Al (*stunned, quiet*)   Elinor . . . are you saying if he hasn't done it, at least he's near, *so it doesn't matter if he's forged the results . . . ?*

Elinor   *You* are saying he hasn't done it – I am saying I know he is near.

Al   I can't believe you mean that, Elinor.

Elinor   I do mean it.

Al (*erupting*)   For Chrissake, if we start thinking like that, everything goes, doesn't it. Everything we believe in!

Moving rapidly.

One can announce I've discovered a cure for all forms of cancer, or AIDS, or I've saved the world from a new killer bacteria . . . I have! I truly have! Well, *almost*. In fact, what I should have said is I *nearly* have – except I've cheated. I've forged a few results along the way – IN FACT IT'S ALL A FAKE.

Elinor (*steely*)   I'm not saying that, Albie – and you know I'm not.

Al (*disbelief*)   No?

Elinor   I'm saying there are things here you don't understand.

Al   That's true!

Elinor   And by giving them time, they'll clarify themselves.

Al   You are saying ignore it, *even* if I have evidence. I CAN'T BELIEVE you are arguing that, Elinor, you've spent your whole life setting standards, being an example to others –

Elinor   I've spent my whole life resisting obvious explanations, because they are invariably wrong. (*She looks up*.) I've had to learn the importance of waiting –

Al (*suddenly*)   It's a con, don't you realise. An idea that sounds so pure, sunlight and water, is a fucking con. He's used baking powder, for Chrissake! It's as crude as that. As sleazy as that.

Elinor (*implacably*)   I don't believe it. That is totally impossible. Quite impossible. (*Pause*.) That certainly hasn't happened.

Silence. She looks at him, sound of the computer games outside.

Albie, I have known you nearly half your life. I have taught you.

Al (*quiet, watching*)   Tried to teach me.

Elinor   Tried to teach you, yes. (*Smoking.*) I probably
know you as well as anyone – and I'm telling you this is not
the time to intervene. There will be a professional and
scientific explanation, of that I'm certain.

Al   Will there?

Elinor   I am convinced there will be. But if you blunder in
now, with your flair for popularising things –

Al   Yes. I know I'm a hack, but that's not the point –

Elinor   – you will generate all kinds of media coverage,
naturally. And that will have a devastating effect on
Christopher's reputation . . .

Al   And if it comes out I had prior knowledge of the
deception –

Elinor   There has been no deception, Albie.

Al   If it comes out I had proof and did nothing –

Elinor   Yes?

Al   Then the whole department is finished. That doesn't
matter?

Elinor   I don't think you have a choice, Albie. (*Silence.
Softly.*) Do you understand the situation better now?

Al   Yes. You're forbidding me from doing anything.

Elinor   Don't be silly, Albie – how can I forbid you. That's
childish. (*Silence.*) Come here . . .

Al *moves up to her. She touches his hair, her tone much more gentle.*

Elinor (*softly*)   You look awful, unwashed, unkempt.
(*Looking at his shirt.*) This is filthy.

Al   Yes, I've been sleeping in my clothes. There's probably
a special mould growing here – a new strain of penicillin.

Elinor *suddenly intense, the whole strength of her personality.*

Elinor   I'm telling you – from all my experience from
everything I've learnt – I'm telling you . . . you must not act.
You must not do it.

Pause. The computer sounds, lazy rhythms, music drifting.

(*Gently.*) You've got many qualities, Albie, you've got to concentrate on what you do best, what comes naturally – your gift for organisation, for planning.

Al (*quiet*)   Yes.

Elinor   Are you going to listen?

Pause.

Al   Yes.

Elinor   Good. That's good. (*She moves.*) Come on then, chip chop. We've a picnic to attend. (*She smiles.*) Imagine them all lying in the long grass, guzzling. If we leave it any later, they'll have eaten all the food. (*She moves.*) We can go in my car.

Al   No. I just need a moment to see to something. I'll drive myself. I know where it is.

Elinor   OK, right. Super. (*She moves to exit.*) See you under the trees. (*She exits.*)

Al alone. He moves slowly.

Al (*quiet*)   Jesus . . .

Joanna *enters.*

Joanna   I knew you'd still be here.

Al only looks up.

Joanna   You're not going to the picnic, are you?

Al (*preoccupied*)   What? No I can't.

Joanna   And we're not going away together?

Al (*concentrating deeply*)   What?

Joanna (*laughs*)   Well, that couldn't be clearer. (*Lightly.*) I was stupid to expect anything else, wasn't I?

Al grunts deep in thought.

Joanna   I thought so. I'll have to settle for this. (*Touching him gently.*) Whatever this is. (*She smiles.*) I don't think *this* is very much. (*She moves.*) Sometimes I think you're only interested in me because we met on the day you became Professor — I'm really just a memento, and will end up in a plastic bag. (*She stares at him.*) Come on, Al, what's the matter?

Al *looks up.*

Joanna   Since you're obviously not thinking about me at all.

Al (*quiet*)   No. (*Looking at* **Joanna**, *very preoccupied.*) The old bastard was right. Elinor was no help.

Joanna   You told her about Christopher?

Al   Yes . . . the most scrupulous person I've ever known, the great Elinor — and she told me to do nothing.

Joanna   And what did you say?

Al   I just reverted . . . I couldn't prevent it. I became the pupil again. (*Pause.*)

Joanna   She probably needs a little time to take it all in.

Al   No, *no*. That is not what is happening.

Joanna (*burrowing in her bag*)   By the way, Barbara gave me this notebook — where is it? — a little thing with a rose on it . . . Here, she asked me to give it to you. (*She hands him the book.*) She said you'd understand.

Al   Yes, I was expecting it.

Joanna   Aren't you going to look at it?

Al   I know what it'll show.

He flicks the pages but he's not really looking at it.

It's evidence. She will have written what she saw.

He flicks the pages again, this time looking for longer.

Shit! Yes! (*He lets out a yell of rage.*) I can't ignore this!

Joanna   It's difficult, of course, for you, Al. (*She watches him.*) But you did a piece of detective work – and you came up with a result.

Al   I wasn't expecting to! I really didn't *want* to be right! (*Pause.*) I still don't know why it's happened. (*He paces.*) It's like I've put the pieces of the jigsaw together, and I'm staring at it now, and I don't know what it shows. Except Christopher's finished. *However* it's presented to the world, whatever euphemism is used he's finished.
But I don't know why it's happened.

He moves round the stage.

What do I keep from here? From this bloody morning? (*He moves, intense.*) The day of the celebratory picnic. What lousy little thing should I keep? . . . so I remember *exactly* what it was like.

Staring across at **Joanna**.

I wish somebody would rumble me. Tap me on the shoulder and say OK, that's it. We know you're pint-sized, you're here by accident. *We'll* take care of it from now on. You've done enough. (*He moves again. Then stops.*) Rumble me . . . come on, for Chrissake . . . Rumble me!

Fade.

Act Two

Scene One

Al *facing us, with a larger plastic container at his feet.*

Al   A good place to restart I think, is with this − (*Gives bag a nudge.*) somewhere in the intervening four years I'd graduated to bigger bags . . .

He turns the bag round slowly.

We have gone right past that colour supplement − with us on the cover − and reached this. (*Pulls in stomach.*) Despite my best efforts I'd grown a little fatter too − just a touch. (*Prizing open bag.*) So what do we have . . . ?

He looks inside. Silence.

Strange smells. (*Pause.*) We find a load of audio tapes, of my own voice. Well, why not? A fistful of press cuttings and . . . (*Producing it with a flourish.*) And a fork − pinched from the Garrick Club!

He stares at fork, for a moment.

I was very busy . . . hectic days . . . and in the middle of it all, I kept on getting invited by that old villain Brownhill for lunch at his club. (*He exits.*)

The **Professor** *and* **Joanna** *are sitting side by side in deep armchairs.* **Joanna** *is dressed fashionably but impersonally. She seems older, more sophisticated. She is very ill at ease though, sitting waiting with the* **Professor**.

Professor   You won't recognise him.

Joanna   Won't I? I haven't been away that long!

Professor   As soon as he comes in, you will see a considerable difference. He struts.

Joanna   Struts! Really? I can't imagine Al strutting.

Professor   And God, does he work. Not real work, of course, mostly admin, but he beavers away —

Joanna   Well, he's always beavered, worked harder than he made out.

Professor   His snout in here, his snout in there. I don't resent him. We need his sort. Everybody finds Albert useful — I was right. (*He looks around, smiles.*) You know he gives these little talks on the radio now.

Joanna (*amused*)   He doesn't? What about?

Professor   Oh yes, before the news in the morning. Only five minutes, mind you. (*Slight laugh.*) That's quite long enough for Albert's thoughts! What used to be called the God slot. (*Admiring smile.*) Load of balls, of course.

Al *enters.*

Professor (*totally unfazed*)   There you are. I was just saying, one can't open a newspaper or switch on the radio, without hearing your voice.

Al   Rubbish, William. You exaggerate. (*He stares at* **Joanna**.) Hello, Joanna.

Joanna   Hi, Al.

Al (*warm*)   Hi! (*He leans over and kisses her.*)

Professor   Still to conquer TV, of course. But that will come next no doubt.

Joanna (*as* **Al** *kisses her, whispers*)   I didn't realise we weren't going to be alone.

Al (*whispers*)   I'll explain later. (*Louder.*) You look wonderful!

Joanna   I feel wonderful — ish.

Professor   You won't when it starts filling up here. The members rolling in, muttering to themselves.

Joanna   Well, you certainly look successful, Al.

Al   Do I? (*Intimate.*) You look so different, Joanna.

Professor   He's written a book too, 'Beware of the
Experts', crude but effective, pandering to the young. Gives
us veterans a good hiding. (*He smiles.*) It's selling really well,
of course.

Joanna (*to Al*)   You never sent me a copy.

Al (*intimate, urgent*)   I hope you've kept all afternoon for me,
say you have. *Please*, it's important.

Al, *close to her, touches her arm.*

Joanna (*warm laugh*)   That depends!

Professor   But it's not just media claptrap. He's on a
number of committees too.

Al   Anybody can be on a committee, especially if you offer
to do the minutes —

Joanna   Anything of importance?

Professor   Oh yes.

Al (*embarrassed, laughing*)   Jesus! Stop! He's like my agent,
isn't he!

Joanna   ou have an agent too?

Professor   Albert's on quite a vital committee, grading
science departments in universities round the country —

Al (*broad grin*)   He likes to think 'you see what I've
unleashed on the world'.

Professor   Half horrified of course! (*Chuckling.*) More
than half.

Al (*returning to* **Joanna**, *softly*)   You're marvellously brown,
how did you get to look like this in New York in the winter? Is
this how you look all the time?

Joanna   Oh no, this is just for you, Albert, of course!
(*Suddenly.*) Have you done Fraud, by any chance, in one of
your five-minute talks?

Pause.

Al   A Scientific Fraud? No.

Joanna   No?

Professor   Oh, you mean Christopher – there've been endless articles by all sorts of riff-raff, most of them with awful titles, like 'The Baking Powder Fraud', colour supplement stuff.

Al   But not by me, and not about why it happened, which is the important question, nobody's bothered yet –

Professor (*cutting him off*)   No, Al's not cashed in directly, hasn't written a book about Christopher. But once he found himself in the spotlight, he made damn sure he stayed there, didn't you, Albert?

Al (*startled by this*)   Thank you!

Joanna   Have you *seen* Christopher?

Al   No. (*Slight pause.*) I hear he's managing.

Joanna   He is? And how is Elinor?

Al   (*smiles*) – Oh, she's even more like Elinor than usual – still eating the barley sugars.

Professor   I can tell you what happened with Christopher –

Al *stops, surprised.*

Joanna   You can?

Professor   It's quite simple, he was always a non-entity.

Al   No, that's not the case!

Professor   Oh yes, a non-entity. He wanted to lie his way to the top, because deep down he knew he wasn't good enough.

Al (*anger rising*)   Christopher was not a non-entity!

Professor (*glibly*)   He had a humble background – he was desperate to succeed.

Al (*his anger bursting out*)   That is not true. You want to play this game, solve the mystery, then you have to get your bloody facts right! Christopher's the son of a country doctor, as it happens, a very happy childhood, (*Loud*.) the solution doesn't lie there, I assure you!

Startled pause.

Professor Maybe not, Albert. You're the authority on people, after all. But the result's the same, isn't it. (*He gets up*.) As I get older I get much less forgiving, I'm afraid. (*To* **Joanna**.) I've said my piece, now I must relieve myself. You will excuse me, my dear. Soon you will have the benefit of our gruesome cuisine, overcooked beyond belief. (*As he exits*.) I hope you're not too hungry.

Joanna Thank God he's gone for a moment. I didn't realise he was quite *that* loathsome.

Al That's him on a good day!

Joanna He hates everything, doesn't he? (*She laughs*.) He even hates the food.

Al For some reason he doesn't hate *me* – which is worrying. (*Pause. He stares at her, very warmly*.) So here we are, Joanna. Both pretty *OK*.

Joanna (*smiles*) Yes, that's right.

Al (*intimate, close*) How's the job?

Joanna (*laughs*) I can't believe it! A question about *my* work. It's good – I'm working as a publicist now.

Al A publicist!

Joanna Don't say it like that.

Al The Hype Industry.

Joanna Yes, but it's not just that. We concentrate on the arts. Publishing. (*She smiles*.) Maybe we'll be handling your books.

Al I'm sure. (*He looks at her for a moment*.) That thesis you wrote – 'The Impact of the Invention of Detergent' – that was very memorable, Joanna.

Joanna Memorable! You've never said that before.

Al   Oh yes. (*He grins.*) I often think about it. How we met. You were so confident – you showed great originality in being interested in that.

Joanna   You want something, Al, what is it?

Al (*softly*)   I've missed you terribly.

Joanna   Of course you have, once every eighteen months.

Al   No, no.

Joanna   So much, I didn't even qualify for a meal on my own. (*Very direct.*) So what is it?

Al *lowers his voice.*

Al   I didn't want to say this in front of the Professor, but –

Joanna   Say what?

Al (*glancing round*)   I have to be quick, his pee-breaks are disappointingly short. (*His tone hushed, urgent.*) I may be going to see Christopher very soon. First time since . . . next week, at the university.

Joanna   Great. I'm sure you should.

Al   And I want *you* to come with me.

Joanna (*startled*)   Why? This is surely something you've got to do on your own.

Al   No. I want you to be there. It's important, I have an agenda.

Joanna   An agenda? What does that mean?

Al   I AM GOING TO PUT THE PIECES BACK TOGETHER, before my luck runs out. It's bound to be difficult. Mission impossible maybe. But *I can do it.* Christopher is very practical – I think he sees me as somebody who in fact contained the storm, who didn't call in professionals to break the fraud, but handled it myself.

Pause. He stares at her.

And I need *your* advice really badly.

Joanna   Don't overdo it, Al, it doesn't suit you.

Al   OK. (*Slight pause, he smiles*.) I'm too much of a coward to do it on my own. Is that better?

Joanna   Yes. (*She smiles warmly*.) That's a little better.

Blackout.

Scene Two

The green faded walls of the department. Two vending machines, now, the old sixties one, and a much newer model, it's neon display shining out. Cafeteria tables, chairs upturned on one of them. **Charlie** *standing behind service area.* **Elinor** *is eating out of pudding bowl.*

Elinor   A little more custard, Charlie.

Charlie   That's your third one, Dr Brickman.

Elinor (*lightly*)   Don't argue, just go ahead and do it. And make it a big dollop, this time, no – *bigger*. (*She smiles*.) Super. Thank you.

Joanna *enters*.

Joanna (*quiet, tentative*)   Hi, Elinor . . .

Elinor *turns*.

Elinor (*startled*)   Oh, goodness . . . (*Moment's pause*.) Hello, stranger. What brings you here?

Joanna   I'm not sure. (*Nervous laugh*.) I mean, Al is here, he wanted me to come. I'm sorry – of course I'm *glad* to be here.

Elinor (*eating her custard*)   There's no need to apologise, we're delighted to see you, aren't we, Charlie?

Charlie   Delighted.

Joanna   I'm not disturbing you?

Elinor   No, no, this is my custard break. Every evening at the same time, lots and lots of it.

Charlie   She's becoming addicted.

Elinor   Absolutely. (*Calmly, easily.*) The most attractive man I've ever met – so far – happened over a shared bowl of custard . . . it's always been a very sexy substance for me.

Joanna (*startled laugh*)   Elinor, I'm surprised.

Elinor   Yes. (*Eating custard.*) In fact I've started a campaign – Charlie and I are planning to reintroduce all the desserts and sweets of our childhood into this cafeteria, aren't we . . . gobstoppers and tons and tons of sherbet. (*She smiles.*) Gleefully putting the clock back.

She looks up from her bowl of custard.

So where is Albie?

Joanna   He's just coming. Any moment. He's been rushing around visiting people.

Elinor   We haven't seen him for a while, he's been very occupied I believe with his articles, his books, his talks. (*Very deadpan.*) I heard one actually, a radio talk, it was about a weighty and important topic – why cats' urine, or should I say cats' piss, smells so much.

Charlie *laughs.*

Elinor   No it was.

Charlie   As bad as that! He has fought for the department though, hasn't he, protected it.

Elinor   Yes. Well, that is what he's there for.

Charlie   Managed to limit the damage after the Occurrence.

Elinor (*slight laugh*)   Charlie always refers to it as the 'Occurrence'.

Charlie   Yes. And the Occurrence is over now – the effects. I'm sure they are.

Joanna   Christopher's meant to be coming, isn't he?

Elinor   Well, if Albie is here, I doubt it. But one never knows. Christopher travels a lot, his arrangements change.

Joanna (*watching her closely*)   And how are things here?

Elinor   Good. Very good. (*She looks up.*) You know, Charlie and I – we've been here the longest of anyone. Charlie six months less than me.

Charlie   'Fifty-seven. I was here in May 'fifty-seven.

Elinor (*laughs*)   And you looked ancient even then!

Charlie   Yes, well, it means I haven't changed, doesn't it! Of course it was a sit-down service then, rather grand.

Elinor (*putting custard bowl down*)   That was delicious.

Joanna   Have you finished your work?

Elinor *stops.*

Elinor   I haven't finished, no.

Joanna   Are you near?

Elinor (*lightly*)   You sound like Albie.

Joanna   I didn't mean to pry.

Elinor   No, it's fine – sometimes it seems jolly near, and other moments I'm not so sure. But in a few months, probably, something will appear. I still stalk the passages at night, don't I, Charlie?

Charlie   Yes, I see her pass by, just as I leave for the night.

Al*'s voice in the passage, calling out, greeting someone.*

Elinor   Oh, goodness, so there he is already. (*Pushes chair into the table. She moves in opposite direction.*)

Joanna   What are you doing? Don't go. He's coming to see you.

Elinor   I know. I'm not avoiding him, I promise. (*She smiles.*) But my custard break is over. And Albie is much better faced in the morning, that's always been the case. (*She exits.*)

Al *enters, a second after* **Elinor** *has exited. He's carrying a large black rubbish bag, stuffed with papers.* **Al** *looks around, surprised.*

Al   I thought for a moment –

Joanna   Elinor was here. She was. She had to go. She's looking forward to seeing you in the morning.

Al grunts, puts the rubbish bag down on the table, papers pouring out of it.

Joanna   What's that grunt mean?

Al   One moment, I just need to, these are some of my old papers, just checking . . . Just refreshing. (*He is lost in thought.*)

Joanna   What is this? What's so important suddenly?

Al lets out a grunted 'Just one moment'.

Joanna (*lightly*)   This is some compliment! (*To* **Charlie**.) He begs me to come with him and then he does this! Hello? (*Moving close, touching him.*) What's going on, Al?

Al grunts, hardly audible, 'one more minute'.

Joanna (*laughs*)   Thanks! Of course, that explains everything. (*She moves.*) To think I let the last precious moments of my 'youth' dribble away among the smells of this department. (*To* **Charlie**.) No disrespect intended! (*Touching* **Al**'s *head.*) But I was rewarded by witnessing something special. (*Slight pause.*) Not today!

Al grunts.

Joanna   Tonight of all nights – he starts playing the mad professor! Oh, Al.

Al (*sharp*)   Just one moment please, I just have to . . . (*His voice tails away.*)

Joanna (*lightly*)   Fuck it. (*To* **Charlie**.) If he ever notices I've gone – I'll be in the bar.

She exits. **Al** *doesn't see. Silence.* **Charlie** *having his cigarette break, standing by the food.*

Al (*with papers*)   Forgotten how to do this, it's been so long. I have to stick my tongue out to concentrate, like a school-kid. (*Suddenly looks up.*) Joanna?

Charlie   She went.

Al   She went? (*Slight pause.*) That helps for a moment. (*His tone changes, more expansive.*) Do you believe in Eureka moments, Charlie?

Charlie   You mean moments of sudden discovery, sir?

Al   Yes, like in a cartoon – the light bulb coming out of a head, bang! (*He smiles, looking at* **Charlie**.) A moment like that?

Charlie   I'm not sure I've ever seen one, sir. (*Laconic grin.*) Despite all the eminent talent that's filed right past me in this cafeteria.

Al   Nor have I. Till now. (*He gets up.*) This is not strictly speaking a Eureka moment.

Charlie   What? (*Grins.*) There is one happening in here – now? (*Startled.*) With you, sir?

Al   Amazing as it may seem, yes. It's not a pure Eureka moment – because I've had this idea for several weeks, ever since I found these old notes of mine – from my younger self, surprisingly bright in fact. They got me thinking . . .

Pause, he moves round the formica table.

But this is the nearest I'll ever get to a Eureka moment. (*He flicks papers.*) Let me see if it works again.

Charlie   Shall I get anybody else to witness this?

Al   No, no. This is just for you, Charlie. I'm not ready for a bigger audience. This *is me* doing it, after all! (*He stands by table.*) It doesn't sound very prepossessing – it is to do with GARBAGE. Rubbish, waste . . . (*Looks at* **Charlie**.) no obvious jokes please.

Charlie   Did I say anything, sir?

Al   *Garbage* – extracting workable fuel, a form of petrol, from household waste. That you can run vehicles on. It is not quite as big an idea as the Sun Battery, but it could be very important. (*Smiles.*) Maybe. (*He moves to table.*) Give me that please, Charlie.

He takes ladle, and scoops some baked beans straight out onto the table, beginning to form a diagram with them, smudging them across the table-top.

If this is the raw material, one would have to grind it . . . grind (*He does so to the beans for a moment, smashing them with ladle.*) then . . . (*He takes some mushy peas, expands the diagram.*) then mix with water containing the catalyst, the vital rhodium catalyst . . . and then . . . give me those burgers, Charlie.

He ladles some very overcooked burgers onto the table, and into the diagram.

You add hydrogen gas and then the co-catalyst phosphine. (*He ladles some sweetcorn on.*) Do you see the shape? The shape, Charlie? (*He moves with ladle.*) Allow it to cool, release the pressure.

He sprinkles some chips on top.

And the fuel will be floating on the top. Like so . . .

He sprinkles more chips.

Like so. Give me some more . . . more burgers, Charlie . . . they're cooked to a crisp, aren't they! . . . more mushy peas . . . if we could.

He stares at the table-top.

If only we could . . .

He sprinkles some more chips.

It is, of course, round the mushy peas that it is still unclear, it is incomplete. If I put in a lot of work round the mushy peas, Charlie, it will become clearer, it will be achieved.

Charlie   It sounds fantastic.

Al (*grins boyishly*)   It *could* be fantastic.

Music in distance. **Elinor***'s music.*

Charlie   An apple-falling-off-a-tree moment?

Al   No, not quite, Charlie. (*He smiles.*) Undoubtedly the messiest Eureka moment there's ever been . . . I think we can claim that prize!

Charlie   We could still celebrate, couldn't we? You deserve a drink. Shall we go to the bar, sir?

Al   That's an excellent idea, Charlie. But I need to do this now – if I'm going to get it ready for the others.

He moves to end of table with papers.

Have to find a space where there are no beans.

He sits studiously at end of table. **Elinor***'s music in background.*

It's funny, when the place is coming to an end – this happens.

Charlie (*sharp*)   Coming to an end?

Al   I shouldn't have said that. You didn't hear me. The committee has made some decisions but nothing is official. *You* won't be affected, Charlie. But I may no longer have to concern myself with this place. (*He smiles.*) The weight is lifted. (*He works with papers.*) I plan to involve the others with this idea, of course.

Charlie   Dr Christopher and Dr Elinor?

Al   Yes. Form a unit, with them, somewhere else. It'll be a powerful set up. (*Bending over papers.*) This is real work, Charlie, for a change! Do you hear Elinor's music? (*He is writing.*) Do you think Christopher will come?

Charlie   I expect so. He'll want to see you, after all this time.

Al   I'm not sure he'll *want* to exactly! But he'll be curious. (*He smiles.*)

Charlie, *cleaning up, begins to wipe the table, the baked beans diagram.*

Al   Don't, Charlie, leave it! I need that! Don't wipe anything please! Put those back at once, (*He grins.*) I'm using it.

Charlie *flicks beans off the cloth, back onto the table.*

Charlie (*amused*)   I beg your pardon, sir, forgive me.

Al (*more serious*)   If it could work, Charlie, Jesus!

He begins to write.

I'm trying to get it into a presentable form for tomorrow so they can give their comments. Elinor's a very tough judge, of course.

Pause.

Being able to hear her music, it's like you can sense her thought process. I'll work all night if necessary.
I am here, and she is working just down the passage. It's as if we're working in unison for the first time.

Blackout.

Scene Three

Elinor's *laboratory. A portion of the scientific apparatus she uses comes on. It looks almost sculptural, as it bends along one side of the stage. From outside come the sounds of students' parties, from other buildings in the university. At the beginning of the scene the sound is quite faint, a gentle noise of distant music. It is early evening, of the following day, the sun is reddening, then going down during the scene, and various lamps are switched on, dotted around* **Elinor**'s *lab.*

Ghislane *is standing with* **Christopher***. There is a contrast in their manner, even the colour of their clothes.* **Ghislane** *in dark colours, nervous, fidgety, her hair has begun to turn grey.*
Christopher *in a summer suit, and in a seemingly expansive, confident mood.*

Christopher   It's amazing.

Ghislane   What is?

Christopher   That old bicycle with the broken front wheel is still there – after all this time. (*He turns.*) I saw Bogle just now, he's lost almost all his hair.

Ghislane   I don't think I've ever been in here before,
Elinor never encouraged visitors.

Sound of **Al***'s voice in passage.*

(*Nervous.*) She'll be here, won't she? I thought Elinor said she
definitely was going to be here, for the moment when we met
Al.

Christopher (*very calm*)   She'll be here. I saw her earlier
today – (*He laughs.*) we had an orange juice together – she
doesn't change.

Al *and* **Joanna** *enter.* **Al** *is wearing stylish clothes, a rather
fashionable tie. Silence for a split second.*

Christopher   Al.

Al   Christopher.

Christopher (*bantering tone*)   Nice tie!

Al (*grins*)   Well, it's a reunion tie. (*Smiles.*) For *this* reunion.
I spent a ridiculously long time choosing it.

Ghislane   Hello, Joanna.

Joanna   Hi.

Christopher (*casually*)   Yes, hello. (*Only focusing on* **Al**.)
Have you had your hair tinted, Al? I think you have.

Al   No, I have not!

Christopher   It looks lighter, a little tint definitely.

Al (*laughs*)   I have not had it tinted!

Joanna   Unless somebody did it in your sleep.

Al   Must be the sun.

Christopher *watching him.*

Christopher   Yes, I hear it's been a good spring in
England. For once.

Al   Yes. So far. April's been very good, May has started
well. (*Suddenly.*) We're not going to talk about the weather,

are we? (*Laughs*.) Fucking hell – we meet again and talk about the WEATHER.

Christopher (*lightly*)   But you're very good at talking about the weather – aren't you, Al?

Al   What do you mean?

Ghislane   The only one of your radio talks we've heard –

Christopher   Was about the weather.

Ghislane   I think its theme was – contrary to popular belief we don't talk about the weather ENOUGH. (*She smiles*.) It was quite impressive, very confident.

Al (*smiles*)   Confident bullshit, yes.

Pause.

Christopher   And in Japan, I was browsing in a bookshop, when suddenly your perky face was staring back at me, it was your book 'Beware of the Experts' – in Japanese.

Al   In Japan! Really? (*Self-mocking laugh*.) It was probably remaindered, wasn't it?

Christopher (*easily*)   Must be a very different sort of lecture tour, promoting pop-science books.

Ghislane   Plenty of good hotels.

Al   Yes . . .

Joanna   And girls no doubt. Plenty of them!

Al   No, no, I'm planning to settle down. My daughter – who is a real young lady now – doesn't approve.

Christopher (*lightly, ignoring this*)   Bad science – great sex. Al's little buttocks going up and down in hotel rooms all over the world.

Al (*laughs*)   Maybe we should get back to talking about the weather, quick!

Silence. **Al** *moves.*

Christopher . . . Did you get a chance? (*He stops.*) Did you find an envelope pushed under your door this morning?

Christopher An envelope. (*Lightly.*) I might have done.

Pause.

Al So have you had time to look at it?

Christopher *clicks his fingers,* **Ghislane** *produces tape-recorder.*

Al What's that for?

Christopher Just for the record.

Al What record?

Ghislane So everything is absolutely clear.

Christopher No possibilities whatsoever of any distortions.

Al What?

Ghislane It is *my* advice. My legal advice.

Al (*disbelief*) We can't talk with this here – it's like a police interview.

Christopher (*calmly*) Well, that's rather appropriate, isn't it, Al – I saw you described somewhere as a science policeman.

Al Christopher. (*Pacing.*) We don't need it, we really don't . . . this is *you and me*.

Christopher (*calmly*) We just don't want you misrepresenting this conversation in anyway – for popular consumption. (*He smiles.*) It's no big deal, you'll soon forget it's there.

Al Jesus! OK, it stays. For the moment. (*He moves, slight laugh.*)

Silence.

So what do you think? Of the idea? What do you *really think*?

Slight pause.

Christopher   Fuel out of household garbage? Using those two catalysts . . . the rhodium and . . . (*He stops.*) you want my honest opinion?

Al (*very quiet*)   Yes.

Slight pause.

Christopher (*slow smile*)   I think it has possibilities.

Al (*startled*)   Really? You do!

Christopher   Yes . . . it's a sketch at the moment, of course.

Al   Yes, yes! (*He laughs.*) I will type it up properly, re-present it.

Christopher   But it *is* a genuinely good idea.

Silence.

Joanna   That's great, isn't it, Al. (*Affectionate laugh.*) An idea of your own!

Al (*quiet*)   Yes – it's tremendous. (*Pause. His tone urgent.*) I tell you what I want to do, I want to form a UNIT to help develop the idea – and *others*.

Christopher *smiles.*

Al   Please listen to this. (*He moves.*) Do *you* want to be involved? (*He grins indicating the tape-recorder.*) With or without a constant record.

Christopher (*quietly*)   Involved in your unit?

Al   You could rework the Sun Battery, explore further, keeping it rather low profile at first, of course . . . but *after a time* . . .

Christopher, *distant smile.*

Al   I want it to be a powerhouse, a real Powerhouse of Ideas, Christopher.

Elinor *enters.*

Elinor   Oh, good, everybody's here already. (*She smiles.*) I've missed all the awkward bits.

Al   That's right!

Christopher   You're in time for something else, though.

Al   Hi, Elinor.

Elinor   Albie. (*Slight pause.*) It's very good to see you.

Al   Yes – and it's a lovely idea to have this meeting in *your* lab, because I've hardly ever been allowed in it before.

Elinor   So you keep reminding me, Albie. (*Pause. She glances around.*) Well, we all look much the same, don't we? That's rather refreshing – no shocks. (*She smiles.*) Or maybe it's a little disappointing, perhaps we should have all changed dramatically! (*She moves.*) Anybody want some coffee?

Al   Yes, I'll make it.

Elinor   No, no, it has to be found first. It's kept in a disgusting old tin in the passage – (*She smiles.*) to deter anybody from stealing it. It needs me to find it. (*She moves, glancing at* **Al** *and* **Christopher**.) A little coffee, and then we can all start to function properly. (*She exits.*)

Silence.

Christopher (*calm smile*)   Albert – it may seem a charming thought to try to put the pieces together, but the last thing, the very last thing I want is for you to have any control over my actions – as a moment's thought might have told you.

Al   I wouldn't have control –

Christopher   And it's not necessary either. Nothing has *changed* for me.

Al   Nothing has changed?! Come on, Christopher.

Christopher   Not when one looks at the *facts*.

Al   You don't have to pretend here, please.

Christopher   Pretend! What kind of word is that? There is no pretence.

Ghislane   What Christopher means is – things are almost repaired, after a long process of –

Christopher (*cutting her off*)   I know what I mean. (*His tone effortlessly calm.*)   No, I have no need for any of this, Al, but I'll be very interested if you repeat your offer to Elinor, (*Looks straight at him.*) since one of the main reasons you are here, is to tell her you're shutting down her lab – terminating her.

Joanna   What? What is this, Al?

Al   It's not as simple as that. Elinor and I have to have a talk –

Christopher   Clearly.

Ghislane   That's one way of putting it.

Al   – and I have to tell her about the unit, of course.

Joanna   So that's why you were so eager for me to be here with you – because you knew there was going to be unpleasantness.

Al   No! I wanted us all to meet again for several reasons, but primarily to see if we could *resume*.

Joanna   Jesus, Al, I can't believe this! I thought I'd come to watch things being mended, at a reunion.

Christopher *suddenly looks at her.*

Christopher (*very calmly*)   I'm sorry, but you didn't, you came out of voyeurism, didn't you? To see what I looked like now.

Joanna (*startled*)   What?

Christopher   To see how I appeared. (*He smiles.*) It's perfectly understandable.

Joanna   Thanks! (*Nervous laugh.*) I think I can do without this! (*She moves.*) OK . . . ?

Christopher There is absolutely no need to be upset. I'm not in the least angry you came. I would have done the same.

Joanna No. I shouldn't be here. I don't belong here now. (*Moving off.*) Al, please think about what you're doing.

Al It'll be *all right. Don't worry* . . .

Elinor *enters with a battered old tin.*

Elinor Coffee, at last. And we can pig ourselves on ginger biscuits.

Al Great.

Joanna Elinor, I just need to do something, I'll be back soon . . . OK.

Elinor Don't be long.

Joanna *exits. Slight pause.*

Christopher It turns out Al has a couple of things to put to you, Elinor.

Elinor Oh, good. I usually react with interest to what Albie has to say.

Christopher This is of particular interest. And while he's doing that, I think I have some calls to make.

Al You're not going too?

Ghislane (*hastily*) Yes, we have a flight to Germany tomorrow. He's been working very hard.

Christopher Of course. I'm truly busy. There have been times recently when I've just put the phone down, and it has rung immediately, without even a second's delay. I have invitations bulging through the letter-box every morning. (*He smiles.*) Funnily enough, I even get invited to places I was never invited to before.

Al Christopher –

Christopher Maybe out of notoriety, who knows. My life has never been quite so full (*He grins.*) which is odd, isn't it! That's what you did, Al – and I'm not even angry.

Al   I think I'd feel happier, if you were screaming at me.

Christopher   There is no need for that. You thought you had a job to do, it could have done harm, but it *did* not.

Al (*impatient, urgent*)   Christopher, for God's sake! This is me here . . .

Christopher   No, the truth is, listen to the truth, Al, because it's interesting – a temporary adjustment to my career was required, that's all. I bear no ill will, even to that girl, I can't remember her name now, who thought she had evidence. If time and money had allowed, maybe I should have sued, and cleared up everything in the courts. But the moment's passed.

Ghislane (*trying to stop him*)   We better check our departure times now. (*She moves.*)

Al   Christopher! *I want to know why?*

Christopher (*calmly turning*)   I know you want an admission, a confession even. But there is nothing to admit, Al. I just couldn't repeat the experiment, that's all. (*He moves.*) It's very simple really. (*He smiles.*) Don't think about it any further. I know it's galling – *but there is nothing more to discover.*

He exits with **Ghislane**. *Pause.*

Elinor   Well, they certainly don't want to drink my coffee. (*She smiles, looks at disgusting tin.*) Maybe it's the container.

Al   He was amazing – he did it so effortlessly. (*Pause.*) He was so like Christopher! Never letting the mask slip.

Elinor   He was bound to be like that. Naturally, seeing you again.

Al   Yes, of course.

Elinor   It may change in time between you and him. You never know.

Al   It will.

Elinor (*watching him*)   So the sole reason for this visit, Albie, is for you to see Christopher?

Al   Yes – and you, of course.

Elinor *stares across at him for a second. Her manner soft, and informal, seemingly on her best behaviour for* **Albie**.

Elinor   Oh yes, to see *me*. (*She puts down tin.*) I've got a better idea. (*She moves to cupboard.*) I have a bottle of whiskey somewhere.

Al   A drink – in here! In the lab?

Elinor   Oh yes.

Al   That's very unlike you.

Elinor   Oh no, it's not. (*She smiles.*) There's a lot you don't know. (*Pouring whiskey into china cups.*) And it goes with the music – the pre-exam parties. The kids, hear them, last chance to indulge. That's the American film club's party.

Al   You can tell the different parties – just by listening!

Elinor   Yes. I've been working in this room so long, some of the music I used to hear out there has come back into fashion. I suddenly find myself transported back to the sixties.

Al   You should have taped the sound of all those parties through the years, be an incredible record!

Pause. He watches her, clears his throat.

Did you have a chance to see the paper I pushed under the door early this morning?

Elinor   I received it, yes.

Slight pause. **Elinor** *drinking, already refilling cup with more whiskey.*

Al   I gave you the original. (*He smiles.*) That's why it was spattered with beans – I hope that didn't put you off.

Elinor   Oh, it was baked beans, was it – I thought it was chicken curry. Anyway, I got it, complete with the beans.

She moves bottle of whiskey, points to floor.

You see this – it's a very important stain, Albie. Crucial, the biggest here. Trifluoro-acetic Acid. It's from 1967, when a very stormy love affair ended – rather suddenly! Yells and tears . . . (*She smiles.*) The end of several relationships are marked all over here in fact, by different stains. (*She smiles.*) The exact size depending on how intense they were! There's a whole patch just where you're standing! (*She laughs.*) One could crawl on all fours around here in fact, and inspect my private life. (*Pause. She looks up at* **Al**.) Some other time, maybe?

Al (*casually, not interested*)   I must take a look, Elinor, yes. (*Suddenly unable to wait any more.*) So what do you think of the work, my paper? Tell me!

Pause.

Elinor (*smiles*)   Your 'paper' – what I saw of it, through the baked beans?

Al   Yes?

Elinor   I thought it was great.

Al *takes this in for a second, disbelief. Pause.*

Al   It is? Isn't it? (*Punches the air.*) Yes! (*He moves, excited.*) Never heard you call anything great before.

Elinor   Maybe super, rather than great. Naturally it needs work – there are obvious gaps.

Al   Of course, yes . . . but as a start?

Elinor   It's more than a start.

Al   Yes? This is terrific . . . Elinor, isn't it?

Pause. The sound of the parties.

Elinor   Was it, how shall I put this – all your own work Albie?

Al (*lightly*)   Amazing as it may seem, yes.

Elinor   Nobody else contributed?

Al   No.

Elinor (*sipping whiskey*)   Are you sure? Before the baked beans stage – there was nobody else?

Al   Jesus, what is this? (*Nervous laugh.*) You think I stole it? You can't believe that, Elinor. (*Moves.*) After all, it's not *me* who was found to be doing fraudulent experiments.

Pause.

Elinor   No, Albie. *That* you haven't done.

Al   What does that mean?

Elinor   No, no, I'm on my best behaviour tonight. (*Looking across at* **Al**.) I'm trying to do myself some good here, aren't I?

Slight pause. She drinks. **Al** *turns.* **Elinor** *lightens her tone.*

Hear that? It's another party starting . . . that's the poetry society. The music's always very violent there.

Al (*calmly*)   Please, Elinor – you must tell me exactly what you mean. You can't think I got it wrong about Christopher?

Elinor   No. (*She moves to equipment.*) I've just got to do this . . . I am prepared to accept there were irregularities.

Al   Irregularities!

Elinor   That Christopher had a complete aberration. That I was wrong.

Al   And I was right.

Elinor *by equipment.*

Al   Can I help? Can I be of assistance?

Elinor (*taking a sharp reading*)   No. I've done it. (*She turns.*) What I cannot accept, I have to tell you, is the way you have used what has happened – how everything that followed your discovery about Christopher has been passed off as a complete accident – but each time it's led to your advancement in some way.

Al   I've only been doing what I've always done, Elinor, keeping my head above water. You know that's how it's happened.

Elinor   Don't be absurd.

Al   It's the truth.

Elinor (*calmly*)   I don't just mean your silly talks on the radio, but how you've used the wave of anti-science feeling for your own purposes, feeding people's cynicism. And fear. According to you, not only are scientists solely responsible for buggering up the planet –

Al   I don't believe that.

Elinor   But a great number of them aren't even any good. Exaggerating the value of their work to get funding, et cetera, et cetera. And you've become a best-selling author peddling that – it's brilliant! And a little nauseating.

Al (*watching her*)   Go on.

Elinor   You've always described yourself as a hack, Albie – but now you've become slightly more dangerous. Somebody who reduces everything to their own level – and does it very effectively.

Al   My rise, Elinor – if it can be called that – *is* an accident, one haphazard thing, after another.

Elinor   Of course.

Al   I'm not upset.

Elinor (*more softly*)   It takes a lot more to upset you, Albie, I know. (*Sipping whiskey.*) Keep drinking . . .

Al   And it will not influence me, in any way.

Elinor   No?

Al   I will just point out you haven't seen an awful lot of me recently.

Elinor (*very sharp, suddenly*)   Oh, but I think I have, haven't I! Oh yes, very definitely.

Al   What you mean, I haven't been here. What you talking about?

Elinor   On the rare occasions I venture out, I see you all over the place, slices of you, Al.

Al   What?

Elinor   Things that remind me of you – staring at me from the sides of buses, from giant posters. One can't move anywhere without being urged to tailor things to the market-place, justify everything in commercial terms. (*She moves.*) I see you everywhere, Al, and I dread seeing you.

Al (*louder*)   That is not true!

Elinor (*more lightly again*)   Maybe you should reach the other thing you've come to tell me, Albie.

More new music and party sounds.

Al (*slowly, deliberately*)   Elinor, when I started being in charge here, my attitude wasn't entirely formed. What I've experienced at first hand since then, has left me in no doubt that most work should be geared directly to the market-place . . . But it is a really crude analysis to think that's *all* I believe in.

Elinor (*with her back to him, listening to the parties*)   Is it?

Al   It's a caricature to say I'm just crassly commercial. *I* was the one who told Christopher to slow down. (*Suddenly.*) AND YOU TOLD ME – UNFORGIVABLY – TO IGNORE WHAT I'D FOUND. TO FORGET IT.

Elinor   You misunderstood what I said, no doubt for your own reasons.

Al   No. It still stuns me when I think about it, what you told me to do.

Elinor   If that's what you want to believe.

Al   That's what happened, for Chrissake – THOSE ARE THE FACTS.

Elinor   If it helps you to think that, to justify your drive for efficiency.

Silence.

Al   Tell me, Elinor, have you had a new idea in twenty-five years?

Pause.

Come on, tell me, I'm interested, a single fresh idea?

Elinor   One or two, I believe, yes.

Al   Name them. Come on, tell me. (*Very sharp.*) Name just one.

Elinor   This is stupid.

Al   All this secrecy, all this proud isolation, which has got even worse recently – and yet there isn't a shred of evidence that anything has been produced here, is there! You can't expect nobody to ask questions. To give you a licence to go on here for ever.

He stops, stares at her.

THE WORK IS SO PURE – IT IS INVISIBLE.

He moves round the equipment.

There is nothing here! That is the truth. Absolutely NOTHING.

Elinor (*calm, defiant*)   If you say so, that must be right. That must be correct.

Al (*loud, powerfully*)   And it hurts, doesn't it, when this blundering hack, somebody who you taught – actually comes along with a fucking good idea. Out of nowhere, without years of work! This complete mediocrity. That hurts like hell, doesn't it. (*Pause.*) What's more, the little bastard can organise things too, can't he! Which none of you can do. Because you *despise* all that.

Silence.

Elinor (*calm, nicotine gum in her mouth*)   For some reason I've always thought one day you'd probably hurt me. (*Looks across at him.*) That I'd suffer physical harm from you.

Al (*contemptuous*)   Don't be ridiculous, that's really ridiculous, Elinor, isn't it? (*Enraged.*) That's truly pathetic.

Pause. The music of the parties.

Elinor   Come on, why don't you do what you've come for anyway?

Al   Do what?

Elinor   Oh, Albie, don't play dumb with me now. You've come to tell me, that because of the conclusions of the committee that you were a member of – you are recommending that this department should be closed down, and the research facilities with it. (*Pause.*) You're not going to hesitate now, are you?

Silence.

Al (*has recovered his calm, watches her for a second*)   I had an idea a few days ago, for a science fiction story, about a nightmare place, a kingdom, where everybody had to sack one person who had been their lover, or best friend. (*Looks at her.*) Or someone who they'd hero-worshipped.

Elinor *snorts at this.*

Elinor   I should make a note of that if I were you – could be the beginning of your career in fiction. (*Pause.*) So?

Al   I will write you a letter.

Elinor   A letter? Really? What will it say?

Music.

Al (*quiet, careful*)   It will say in view of the present financial realities – this particular university will concentrate on its strengths. And therefore it will no longer possess a chemistry department, no new students will be admitted, and the research facilities will close at the end of September.

Pause.

Elinor (*shocked by the date*)   September? I need another year, that's too soon.

Al   I will send you the letter.

Elinor   I need another year, Albie.

Al   That is not going to be possible. This is nothing personal, it is happening in many areas.

Elinor (*moving*)   I *must* have another year. (*She paces.*) If you need evidence . . . maybe I can let you see something. It's difficult because I'm not ready. I'll have to think about it . . . I don't know if I can. (*She paces.*) It *might* be possible in a few weeks.

Al   Elinor, please, it's gone too far.

Elinor   Do you want me to apologise?

Al   No. *NO*.

Elinor   I haven't been as well as I usually am – had a little trouble with my health . . . apologising is something I do very badly. This is about as well as I do it. Maybe I was a little too severe.

Al   This is not necessary, please.

Elinor (*suddenly looking straight at him*)   You want me to ask in a suitably humble fashion, do you? Is that what you're after? I will. What do you want me to do? – tell me.

Al   Elinor . . .

Elinor   You're a very pragmatic person, Albie, tell me what I have to do, to get the closure postponed? (*Pause. She smiles.*) Shall I really shock you, and plead? . . . I will.

Al, *clearly embarrassed, turns away.*

Elinor (*louder*)   Show me what I need to do? (*She watches him.*) Show me, Albie.

Ghislane *enters.*

Ghislane   Hello, I just came back to . . . (*To* **Elinor**, *sensing the mood.*) I thought we hadn't had a proper moment to say hello.

Elinor (*quiet*)   No, no, we haven't.

Ghislane   Is everything all right?

Elinor   Yes – except I'm drinking too much.

Al (*quieter, now they are in public*)   I will send you the letter.

Elinor   I'm sure you will.

Al (*finding it very awkward, now* **Ghislane** *is there*)   I know you'll find alternative funding, I mean with your reputation, there will be no problem.

Elinor   And of course at my age, it will be even easier.

Al (*moving very close to her, quiet*)   I could make some calls, some suggestions . . . if you want me to.

Elinor   *NO*. I do not. You're right, you send me the letter, Albie. I think that's how it should be. And then you will get my response. (*She moves*.) I'm fairly certain I have never received a letter like that before.

Al (*in exit*)   I *will* see you before I leave.

Al *exits. Pause. The party music playing.*

Elinor   Oh, Jesus! (*Her back to* **Ghislane**, *shaking, really shaking, clenched.*)

Ghislane   Elinor . . . (*Moving up to her.*) I just came, I knew what he was going to say to you . . . I wanted to see if you were all right.

Elinor (*loud, pulling away from her*)   Yes. Of course I'm all right. I told you that. What do you expect me to do – curl up in a heap? (*Pause.*) I didn't mean to shout, I'm sorry. (*She moves.*) I'm not all right of course, but I will see to it that I am.

She stops moving, her composure begins to return.

I still have a great desire to finish the work – and that is what is going to happen. (*Sharp.*) Without a doubt – there's plenty of ammunition left . . .

Ghislane   I can't believe we've let him do this to us, Elinor.

Elinor   I was not aware I'd *let* him do anything . . . I even pleaded with him (*She laughs.*) just now – in my own laboratory – to Albie . . . to little Albert.

She moves, self-mocking smile.

What's more I tried – and this is funny – I even tried to demonstrate my 'passionate' side to him. (*She laughs.*) Oh yes! To show him I wasn't just a woman of uncertain age, all alone in a prehistoric lab, that there was more to me than tins of barley sugars. (*She mimics herself.*) And 'supers' . . . (*She stops moving.*) Everything I've done in my life – whatever my achievements are, my reputation, years of work – and it comes down to me pleading with an administrator. To be allowed to exist!

Ghislane Yes. (*Slight pause.*) And you know Christopher doesn't even hate him.

Elinor Well, at least *he's* been free of Albie's control – since the occurrence.

Ghislane Well, *I* hate Al. I can't help it. But Christopher glides above it all, refusing to acknowledge anything.

Elinor (*quietly*) He shouldn't be like that. He ought to admit to what's happened. The more he denies it, the more it diminishes him. He must face it, or he'll never be able to restart.

Ghislane I know, I have to make him! I will! (*She moves.*) And all the time Al gets more famous. It's extraordinary his rise, his success. I lie awake at night planning revenge Elinor, all sorts of scenarios.

Elinor Revenge . . . (*Lightly.*) Certainly, that would be good. But in fact there is no need to worry about that.

Ghislane What do you mean?

Elinor It's already started. A form of revenge. Because Albie has had an original idea.

Ghislane (*startled laugh*) I heard that – garbage! That's *revenge*?

Elinor Oh yes. It's the first fresh idea he's ever had. And now he's thought of it – it almost certainly won't go away. And that will be very unsettling for Albie.

Ghislane I don't see.

Elinor You will. It's simple. (*She looks across at her.*) He can't finish it on his own.

Blackout.

Scene Four

Al *alone on stage with a large plastic box at his feet. Behind him the sound of Concorde taking off. For a second distant, then passing across the auditorium.*

Al The bags get bigger, the mementoes smaller.

Opens bag and takes out exhibit.

And in here – what do we have? A sachet of garlic mayonnaise as served on Concorde with king prawns! I'm in Concorde a lot. American freebies.

The plane goes overhead, he blocks his ears.

I have had two more pop-science best sellers, the latest called 'The End of Hype' – with a big question mark. It has a rather autobiographical thesis – that on one level Science and the Arts, the old Two Cultures argument have never been further apart, with even the machinery in our homes becoming really difficult to understand. *But* on a deeper level showbiz and science are getting ever closer and closer.

An idea borrowed from Elinor (*He smiles.*) but naturally developed further. (*He moves.*) There's a certain fun to be had from hyping a book with a title like that.

Sound changes.

And now we're in a helicopter flying across the roof-tops of New York. We're aiming straight towards those great glass buildings – like Elinor's Virtual Reality Journey, that night. Heading for a reception in an entirely new building, for the launch of a much publicised new book. Not one of mine for once! (*Pause.*) It is the darkest moment of my life so far.

He is handed a plate, groaning with food.

But the food is great.

Joanna *enters. There is the sound of chatter off, as from a cocktail party. A transatlantic twang in* **Joanna***'s voice. Pile of shiny books on the floor.*

Joanna   There you are! All alone?

Al   That's correct.

Joanna (*laughing at the large plate of food*)   But not without ample provisions.

Al   Naturally. As always.

Joanna   So why did you wander off?

Al   I needed to.

Joanna   What's wrong? You're normally so gregarious.

Al   Because after eight minutes – I'd done that party.

Joanna (*laughs*)   Eight minutes! It took as long as that!

Al (*eating*)   Only minor celebrities in there.

Joanna   You've moved up a league now, have you. Perhaps you have – they have all heard of *you*.

Al (*indicating shiny pile of books*)   And what's more the book is shit.

Pause. Sound of the cocktail party.

Joanna   The book is not shit. (*She smiles.*) It's fucking fantastic. It's a controversial look at the way we live now, the definitive comment on success, to quote the blurb which I wrote.

Al   Oh, come on! We're standing seventy-seven storeys up, celebrating a book about a twelve-year-old boy – who also just happens to be a serial killer. The first child serial killer novel, there had to be one, of course! a perfect book for the dregs of the century.

Joanna   You know everything, Al, of course. And the rest of us are just plain dim.

Al   I didn't say that. But I can tell you how liquid crystal works, and also read all 943 pages of this book, and see right through it.

Sound from the cocktail party. He moves across the stage, tapping sections of the floor.

Let me demonstrate something.

Joanna (*nervous*)   Demonstrate what?

Al   Just have to find the right place.

Pushing the strip of maroon carpet away.

Joanna   What on earth are you doing?

Al   There . . . (*He lifts up a small piece of floor.*)

Joanna   Oh no, Al, you're not going to start pulling the floor up again. (*She laughs.*) You know I still dream about some of the objects you conjured up last time you did this.

Al   We are in a new building, and what do we find, as in all new buildings? (*Pulling up dark cables from underneath the floor.*)

Joanna (*nervous*)   What?

Al   The whole forest of cables, from the computers, waiting to be connected.

Pulling up another cable from a second outlet in the floor, and then another, making them stand up so they dot the stage, standing up firmly, like some strange plants.

Look what's underneath your feet, Joanna . . . !

Joanna   Why are they standing up like that?

Al   Because I'm making them.

Joanna   Snake-charming cables now. They're eerie, Al.

They stare at them.

Al   And in less than a year you'll see them change shape.

Voices from the party.

And those people have no idea what's here, what's in the skirting – do they? In their own offices.

His tone lightens, he moves among the cables.

Joanna You do at least have one real talent, Al – for producing surprises out of the floor.

Al Yes – as *my* blurb says, on *my* dust-jacket, 'I have become a detective patrolling the Zeitgeist.'

He is standing still among the cables, his mood darkening.

Idea for a science-fiction story – the computer cables in a new office building, rustle under the carpets, then they grow, and they rise up, and strangle the occupants, one by one. What do you think? (*Indicating books.*) It's better already than this shit.

Joanna (*watching him closely*) And this omniscience – does it apply to people too?

Al *pushes one of the cables slowly back into its hole.*

Al People?

Joanna Remember them? You see right through people on first acquaintance? Get an accurate print-out just by glancing at them?

Al Sometimes, yes.

Joanna And old friends? You know everything there is to know about them too?

Both moving among the cables, either side of the stage.

Al Yes.

Joanna (*touching a cable*) Like Christopher?

Al He lied – wanted to be famous quick.

Joanna That's it? Just that?

Al Yes. The golden boy had a thirst for money and fame, nothing else.

Joanna (*moving to another cable*) And Elinor?

Al Somebody who no longer could compete. A proud lady who couldn't cope with the modern world.

Joanna   That's her, is it, too? As simple as that?

Al   Yes. Every organisation has at least one, a distinguished employee who becomes outmoded.

Joanna   She will surprise you yet. And me?

Al   You? (*He stares across at her.*) I don't think so. (*He turns.*)

Joanna   Go on. (*Staring at him.*) And me?

Slight pause.

Al (*calm*)   A funny original woman – who in the end settled for being just another PR nonentity.

Pause.

Joanna   Fuck you, Al. (*She moves.*) Don't you dare tell me I could have done more. I have a career, I have control over my life. I will *not* be judged by you.

Al (*very quiet*)   You don't have to believe me

Joanna   You are a complacent little shit, aren't you.

Al (*quiet, dark*)   That's right. Elinor always did say I'd grow up eventually.

Joanna   It's rather frightening the contempt you have.

Al   *We're all hacks now, Joanna.* (*He moves among the cables.*) My great mistake was to think I was in a minority. But now we're all the same. (*He glances up at* **Joanna**.) That's why you and I fit the times so perfectly.

Joanna (*fiercely*)   It must be marvellous to feel like that, to know you understand absolutely everything.

Al   No.

Joanna (*mock astonishment*)   It's not?

Silence. **Al** *not looking at her.*

Al   You remember I had an idea, Joanna – a great idea.

Joanna   Oh yes, something to do with garbage – how appropriate.

Al   Of course, yes. A workable fuel out of refuse, a potentially unlimited supply of energy.

Joanna   Sun Garbage in fact!

Al   Yes. And I'm sixty per cent of the way there – but I can't make it come out. *Nearly, but I can't.*

He stares at the cables.

I shut down a department, a department with a great history, but I could go anywhere in the world with it! Find the commitment, build a team. (*He moves.*) I wanted to involve Elinor.

Joanna   But you didn't have the nerve to ask.

Al   I found it impossible to suggest it to her.

He moves.

I am *tormented* by a good idea, Joanna, that I wish I'd never had! I am in a kind of hell, of planes, parties, bouncing around the world with this in my head. IT WILL NOT GO AWAY.

Joanna   So there is some justice then. Driven crazy by your one good idea, not able to finish it – and hopefully it'll never let go of you.

Al   Oh no. (*Very forcefully.*) If one thing is certain – there will be a solution.

Joanna (*moving towards party*)   I'm going back in there. I didn't think you could hurt me after all this time, Al, but you have.

Indicating cables.

I'll leave you with these – with any luck they *will* rise up and start strangling people.

Al *alone with cables. In the scene change they slide back into their holes as he watches. He exits.*

Scene Five

The bells ringing loudly in the scene change, celebratory bells. Very strong, bright sunlight. **Elinor** *sitting centre stage in full red academic robes. The old* **Professor** *also in academic robes.* **Barbara** *is standing upstage, near vending machine. She is very tanned, expensively dressed. As the bells stop, we can hear the sound of builders working, sporadic drilling and hammering.*

Professor   That noise! It should not be happening now.

Barbara (*moving round, touching the wall*)   Everything seems much smaller than I remember.

Touching the wall by the old drinks machine.

It all seems to have shrunk.

Professor   The builders were meant to stop when the bells started . . . somebody must see to it before the ceremony.

Barbara (*by wall*)   Was it always this colour? Everything seems more muted – after the West Coast light. (*To* **Elinor**, *bending down, raising her voice.*) Are you feeling OK? For your big day?

Elinor   I'm fine. Feeling tiptop.

Barbara (*bending close*)   That's great. And you certainly look it too!

Elinor (*lightly*)   Please . . . Just because I'm getting this honour doesn't mean I've gone deaf suddenly.

Professor   It is so *good* this is happening. (*To* **Barbara**.) The Talbot James Award . . . I think there've only been six other recipients in the whole history of the university – and some of those were undeserved. (*He moves to* **Elinor**.) You're coming out of the shadow of what Barker-Wyatt did, or should I say took credit for. At last! No longer in parenthesis, thank God.

Elinor (*warm laugh*)   Oh, is that where I was all this time? In parenthesis! I never knew . . . that must explain everything.

Professor (*kindly tone*) What I mean is your wonderful contribution is being officially acknowledged, long overdue.

Elinor (*lightly, smoking*) Well, we both agree about that. (*Looking at* **Professor**.) I don't know how you manage it, Bill, but you look younger all the time. (*Lightly*.) It's infuriating.

Professor It's keeping busy and free of worry. I don't have a single responsibility any more! (*He moves to* **Elinor**, *taps her on the shoulder*.) We did the hard work, didn't we . . . (*Indicating* **Barbara**.) All they have to do is follow the path we mapped out. (*He smiles at* **Barbara**.) You know Elinor was always startlingly determined, right from the start.

Barbara I bet she was.

Professor We knew we had to be on top form when she was around, or she'd put us all to shame. We used to call her – I forget why now – we always used to call her (*Taps* **Elinor** *on shoulder*.) the snow tigress.

Elinor Really! (*Very surprised*.) I didn't know that . . . ! I quite like it.

Professor Oh yes. And now this is a very appropriate way for it to end.

Elinor (*turning sharply*) End? Really? Some of us still have work to do.

Professor *and* **Barbara** *glance at each other. Slight pause.*

Professor Of course you do, Elinor. I meant the Department ending . . .

Barbara (*loudly*) Yes. We didn't mean to imply you'd stopped. When do you think you'll publish?

Elinor Very soon, I hope.

Barbara Good, that's very good. And you've arranged where you're going next? (*Slight awkward pause*.) You know I've so much room . . . several spare rooms, you must come and visit me in San Diego one day.

Elinor   Really? That's very kind. I'd like that very much.

Barbara   You would?

Elinor   Yes, when can I come? (*She smiles.*) I'm free in the autumn.

Barbara (*very taken aback*)   So you travel now! You've started flying again? That's good. That's excellent, well done. We must work something out, mustn't we.

Christopher enters with **Ghislane**. *He looks drawn, pale.* **Ghislane** *looks older.*

Christopher   No need to shout for God's sake, why are you shouting at her? She's not deaf.

Barbara   Was I shouting? I'm sorry. (*Nervous smile.*) Must be the excitement.

Elinor (*to* **Christopher**)   Thank you, much appreciated.

Ghislane (*to* **Elinor**)   Hello, you look splendid.

Christopher (*fond smile*)   Of course, she always does.

He completely ignores **Barbara**, *moving up to* **Professor**.

The speeches are usually very embarrassing on these occasions, aren't they. I hope yours will be different.

Professor (*not taking offence*)   Well, it will be no more embarrassing than is normal. Nor will Albert's. (*He lowers his voice, to* **Christopher**.) I'm anxious we get as good a turn-out as we did for Greenslade. They can vary, you know.

Elinor (*overhearing*)   Oh, it's a competition now – who gets the biggest audience for their ceremony! (*She laughs.*) Any empty seats will count against me. I'm not really bothered how many people are there, I promise you.

Professor   It will be full, I'm sure. It's going to be a fantastic day. Albert has arranged everything – so it should go like clockwork.

Ghislane   Al can arrange anything, after all!

Ghislane, *like* **Barbara**, *is nervous, speedy.*

Christopher   I saw Warhurst and Beattie, they looked so much older, I hardly recognised them.

Barbara   It's always a bit of an ordeal coming back to a place, after a long gap, isn't it?

Christopher   An ordeal, is it? *I'm* not finding it so. I feel no worries at all about facing everybody.

Ghislane   Nobody will be thinking about what happened, it's not in anybody's mind.

Christopher   Oh no, on the contrary. I know everybody present will be craning their necks to catch a glimpse – is that really him? How does he look? I don't mind, but it's why a lot of them have come.

Elinor (*amused, smoking*)   And here was I thinking today was about me.

Christopher   Of course! But some of them *will* arrange to bump into me afterwards – (*Mimics surprise.*) 'Oh, there you are, Christopher' – hoping for some dramatic confession. (*His eyes meet* **Ghislane**'s *for a moment.*) Which they are never going to get.

Barbara   And are you still working?

Christopher (*very sharp*)   Of course I'm still working. What do you think I'm doing?

Barbara (*nervous*)   No, no, I didn't mean that . . . I, I, I meant still on the Sun Battery.

Christopher (*dismissive wave of the hand*)   No, no, you are completely out of date. I've moved on, of course.

Barbara   Oh, I see. (*Trying to be friendly.*) I knew you would. (*She moves.*) Remember the day we had the picnic? I often think about it. I remember it really clearly, there was so much food! We were drowning in it, lots of good cheeses, and the weather was really cold, all the autumn leaves everywhere, getting into everything.

Christopher (*suddenly erupting*)   Jesus, you can't even remember that right. Not even that! This is shocking. It was a *summer's day*. A humid day. As if anybody could forget that. You have no memory at all, obviously.

Barbara *is totally shocked at this outburst. Silence.*

Barbara   I, I, could have sworn it was a late autumn day. Surely? We were all huddled up in big coats —

Christopher   *No.* And you were the one taking the photos! (*Contemptuous.*) This is amazing! Or have you forgotten that completely as well?

Professor (*hastily*)   Well, there will at least be a good record of today, a video Albert has arranged, at least three cameras I think.

Elinor   My Talbot James video! (*She laughs.*) Maybe I should collect mementoes like Albie does, something from each of you. (*Looking across at them.*) What would you give me?

Al *enters, smartly dressed, he's holding a walkie-talkie.*

Al   It looks like it's going to be a very good turnout!

Elinor *laughs.*

Al (*surprised by the reaction*)   What's the matter? It's going to be a near record attendance.

Professor   Near record? Excellent!

Al (*bringing cards out*)   I have little seating plans for each of you, with your number, showing you where you all need to go.

Christopher   You've arranged the entire operation, have you?

Al (*smiles*)   Nearly! That building noise shouldn't be going on. (*He speaks into walkie-talkie.*)

Ghislane   You can see to that too?

Al (*grins*)   I hope so! I have stewards outside the hall, if they haven't wandered off. (*Into walkie-talkie.*) John, come in . . . can you see those builders? They're working on the roof of this building, keep them quiet till the end of the ceremony. Use money, lots if necessary.

Professor   Looking after all aspects, splendid!

Al *suddenly turns.*

Al   I want you all to go and check your places, now. Just to make sure where they are.

Al *looking at* **Elinor**.

Barbara   Already? Why?

Al   Then you can come back. Please! *Now*!

Christopher (*calm*)   Of course, Al, whatever you want. (*Begins to move.*) The hypocrisy of these occasions – nobody ever says what they're really thinking, do they. All these fulsome addresses, we're *about* to hear, nobody tells the truth.

Professor   Thank God. Where would we all be if that happened?

Christopher   But wouldn't it be interesting if they really did. Just for once. (*He turns.*) If you did, Elinor . . . TODAY!

Professor   Have you all got your seating plans? (*Trying to sound jocular.*) Let's follow the instructions then, see how near the front we are!

Al   I just have to stay and make sure Elinor is ready.

Elinor (*sharp smile*)   Oh, is that what has to happen?

Barbara (*as she is moved on*)   I really think it's unnecessary for us to do this now. I mean, we're not children! (*Stopping by* **Elinor**.) If I don't see you before, good luck.

Elinor   Thank you, my dear. (*She looks at* **Barbara** *for a second.*) You must try and grow a memory, mustn't you.

Barbara *exits.*

Christopher   Come on, Ghislane – we will do Albie's check, without complaint. (*Very sharply.*) But *I* will be the one who escorts her in. Is that *absolutely* clear. (*To* **Elinor**.) Don't forget what I said, Elinor. (*Softly.*) Make it happen. (*He exits.*)

Ghislane (*nervous laugh*)   We're all so dependent now on Al, we even need him to tell us where to sit! (*She exits.*)

Al   There, it's stopped. The noise.

Professor   Excellent. (*He moves.*) I probably won't recognise this building next time I come here. *Our* department. It'll have a whole new interior. It has seen much fine work. All our endeavours, Elinor! But progress has to have its way. This place's moment has passed. It's unavoidable. It's out of date. Used up.

Elinor (*lightly*)   Are you talking about me, by any chance?

Professor   About all of us veterans, my dear. We old contemplators are not required any more. I include myself. Oh yes! (*He exits.*)

Elinor (*pulling on cigarette*)   Like hell he does. (*Sharp laugh.*) And what's more he is nearly twenty years older than me!

She looks oss at **Al**, *moment's pause between them.*

I can't fi   my hat, Albie. You know, the stupid one with the tassles I l   e to wear. And since you're getting me ready . . .

Al   I'll find it. Don't worry – I'll definitely find it.

Elinor (*watching him as he searches*)   I'm glad it's you in charge of the arrangements today. First you're being at your most charming – and second it means everything will work.

Al   I hope so. I want it to be a stunning occasion, beautiful. (*Quiet.*) One of the best days of our lives.

Elinor (*slight pause*)   Of course.

Taking a drag, blowing smoke.

But Christopher is right.

Al (*surprised*)   Christopher's right? – about what?

Elinor   That nobody tells the truth on these occasions.

Al   But surely it'd be awful if they did.

Elinor   It's like obituaries – they never tell the truth either. (*Calm smile.*) Have you written my obituary yet?

Al (*startled*)   Elinor, what a question! Don't be stupid . . .

Elinor   No, come on now, tell me. I'm sure you've done one for a 'serious' newspaper. After all – (*She laughs.*) They always do them early for people who smoke a lot. And since I'm on eighty a day now, I'm sure to have one! (*Softly.*) What's it like, Albie?

Al (*nervous laugh*)   We can't have this conversation!

Elinor   Oh yes, we can.

Slight pause.

Al   It's good. You'd like it, I think.

Elinor (*slow smile*)   So you *have* written one?

Al   Yes.

Elinor (*laughs*)   I can guess what you've said – keep looking for the hat please.

Al   Yes. (*As he looks.*) I have said this was – is – the life of an important and tremendously gifted scientist, of course! A truly pure practitioner.

Elinor   I don't want to hear the *mush*, I can imagine that, very easily. But what should you have said? – that's much more interesting.

She looks straight at him.

And what should you jolly well have the guts to say today – instead of all the deadly politeness I'm going to get.

Al   I should say . . . (*Slight pause, he looks up.*) my teacher, my idol, had one great lapse when she tried to gloss over an incident of serious scientific misconduct – and things were never the same again.

Elinor   You definitely should say it, during the ceremony. I dare you, Albert.

Al   Many, many times I've wondered, (*Suddenly urgent.*) why did you do that?

Elinor (*calmly smoking*)   That's not difficult – because I was frightened of you.

Al   Oh, come on! That's not true!

Elinor   Oh yes – (*She smiles.*) keep looking for the hat – the idea of having to justify my performance, that was alarming. (*She moves.*) I knew Christopher would be able to save me from all that, *once* he'd achieved his work.

Al   I don't believe you! I can't believe you were frightened!

He, suddenly on an impulse, moves over to the lockers.

This is *not* a serious idea, OK! But maybe we can see something. DON'T LAUGH – you promise.

Elinor   I don't promise anything.

Al (*by lockers*)   There was a moment recently, when I saw things very clearly. But now . . .

He is opening lockers, bulging with transparent bags. **Elinor** *laughs at the sight of them.*

Elinor   Oh no, not those wretched bags again, Albie, please!

Al   Oh yes! Eventually I took over all these lockers, as they became vacant.

He begins to pull out the bags, they stream out.

They're spooky, I know, eccentric yes, a schoolboy habit retained.

The bags are in long glistening lines, tied together, stretching out across stage.

But here they are. (*He grins.*) And if we're not going to be POLITE – then we can use them.

Elinor   God, how many did you keep!

Al   It's all here. I colour-coded them recently – (*He smiles.*) my passion for order. There's blue for when I was very young and –

Elinor   And I started teaching you.

Al   Yes, and then over there, gold for when Christopher made his 'great' discovery.

Elinor   And then *red* for everything that followed.

Al   Yes!

He moves to the glistening lines, beginning to move them to form a pattern.

So look, Elinor — look! — they form a crude diagram you see, an instant pattern of the past.

Elinor   They won't help. They can't show us anything.

Al   They will, they can! We can form any configuration with them — *show why what happened, did*. CAUSE and EFFECT.

Elinor   (*staring at the lines of bags, sharp laugh*)   People will come in from the Assembly Hall and find us playing with plastic bags!

Al holds up a bag.

Al   Look, Elinor — look at this one — it's the day I became professor, it's all caught in here, takes you right back to that moment, instantaneously! Do you remember that afternoon?

Elinor   Yes, of course. Your nosebleed and your new shoes.

Al   (*holding up bag*)   There is the blood stained handkerchief right there.

Elinor   (*staring fascinated for a moment*)   So it is. And I never saw you have another nosebleed, after that day.

Al   I know, remarkable what a little confidence will do.

He moves along the lines, changing the pattern, moving the blue and the black together.

So is the key to everything — WATCH — what happened on that sleepy day? Did I actually *scheme* to stop you becoming Head of the Department, you and Christopher?

Elinor   Yes and no. Nothing is that simple.

Music from the hall begins, slow, ceremonial.

Al I didn't! – I really don't believe I did. I was only trying to survive that interview, to give the old bastard the answers he wanted.

Elinor (*softly*)   And you did that brilliantly, Albie, as always. Forever adaptable. (**Elinor** *flinching at the sound of the music.*) Listen to that pompous music – they only give you these lifetime achievement awards when they think you're no longer a threat . . . (*Sharp laugh.*) when they believe you're already half-dead.

Al *moves shape of the diagram.*

Elinor What are you doing? Try as hard as you can, you cannot reduce what happened to one neat pattern.

Al Oh yes. *Everything is reducible in the end*, if you find the key, and I can. (*Moving along the line.*) We can follow the trail . . . watch . . . through this first day when there were stirrings of resentment and jealousy, because it was the hack that got the job.

Elinor No, that's wrong. Too crude. Because you're not just a hack, Albert. That has never been the case.

Al *looks up very startled. Pause.*

Al I don't think you've ever said that to me before.

Elinor Haven't I? I'm sure I must have . . . in different words.

Al No. Not ever.

Elinor You were one of the brighter people that I taught. You stood out, one of the quickest minds of all. (*She moves.*) What does it matter now? (*Slight laugh.*) Not much can change, can it – not unless I can get out of today, somehow.

Al So here is the vital one – the gold – the great day of Christopher's announcement.

Suddenly urgent.

And I know why he *did it*, now. It wasn't just fame, was it? The primary cause. It wasn't money –

Elinor (*amused*)   Probably not the primary cause, Albie, no.

Al   Elinor, please don't mock. I know, because I've been there as well.

Elinor   Where, Albie?

Al   The hell of creating something. That is, in the dark tunnel you have to be in. THERE IS THE KEY. Christopher couldn't do it because he couldn't be there long enough. He lasted of course much longer than I did. But it snapped. He got so close, upsettingly close, but *something* had eaten away at his stamina. He couldn't bear to be there any more. In that *darkness*.

He stares across at her.

You don't have that problem, Elinor, do you?

Elinor (*lightly smoking*)   This is true – I do not.

Al   The long-distance creator, maybe an endangered species . . .

Pause.

Is that even nearly right do you think?

Elinor   I'm sure it's one of the aspects, yes, Albie.

Al (*loud*)   One of the aspects! Don't do that, it's the TRUTH. Because I know – I've felt it.

Ghislane *enters.*

Ghislane   I forgot our number. Your seating plan.

She picks her way across the bags, staring at them.

Oh, Al – taking these with you? (*She laughs.*) Your unique diary. (*She finds the seating plan.*) Here it is.

She moves, then turns to **Elinor**.

Elinor, I can't bear the idea of facing them all. I know what they'll be thinking.

Elinor   It will be fine, I'm sure. (*Then slightly embarrassed.*) Nobody will be thinking about it.

Ghislane   It will be fine for *Christopher*, I'm sure. He still refuses to acknowledge anything. But for me? You know the picnic that Barbara mentioned. I still have copies of the pictures she took. And the striking thing is – Christopher looks exactly the same now, as he did on that day. It all shows on me, not just my hair, but everything about me, I can feel it when people meet me, they see it all on me! However much I smile and chirp away, they sense it at once. (*Louder.*) And that's never going to change now, is it? (*To both of them.*) And you know it's not. (*Intense.*) *That's what I've got now.*

She moves, glances at **Elinor**.

You *do* look wonderful. (*She takes a deep breath.*) Here goes. (*She exits.*)

Elinor (*with feeling*)   Poor girl.

Al *is quiet.* **Elinor** *stares across the lines.*

Elinor   Where is *that picnic?* The celebratory picnic you didn't attend, Al. That day must be here, scrunched up somewhere.

Al   It's just here (*He gives* **Elinor** *the bag.*) and it's the other great pointer, isn't it? The day when we argued, when you told me to do nothing, which led *directly* to the most stupid decision of my life (*He moves the red line across.*) which I wish I could redraw. *Closing you down.*

Elinor   Yes. (*Surveying the lines.*) It's a haunting shape, Albie.

Al   And it's right.

Elinor   There is one problem. (*She smiles.*) If we're going to use these comic things.

She moves them with her foot.

Al   Yes, you use them. (*He grins.*) We're working together, for really the first time!

Elinor Don't you see, Albie, none of this is the real pattern of what happened. The *only* shape we can be definite about is this . . . (*She picks a bag at random.*) or indeed this . . . (*She chucks it away and picks up another.*)

Al What is it? I don't understand.

Elinor They're all *you*, Albie. The only thing we know for certain is –

She pushes the solitary bag along the stage with her foot.

You were always, *always* going to close me down. Whatever happened.

Al (*immediately*) *No*! That is not right.

Elinor Oh yes! Without Christopher's aberration, and the way I 'shocked' you, without any of that taking place – you would still undoubtedly have done it.

Al You're absolutely wrong.

Elinor (*straight at him*) And of course you would do it *again*. Tomorrow if necessary, with no compunction at all. (*Staring at him.*) Maybe even quicker.

Al No, for Chrissake, Elinor! Are you saying I've learnt nothing. Because that's not true.

Elinor You would do it again for a simple reason – you don't know what I'm doing. And mystery is expensive, infuriating, and uneconomic . . .

Al Oh, come on, Elinor!

Elinor I will not compromise, even now. And you hate me for that.

Al (*shocked*) Elinor.

Elinor Oh yes.

Al I have never hated you. This is rubbish. I admire you more than anybody, passionately, with something akin to love. Of course you must know that.

Elinor You'd still shut me down, Albie. *No problem*, as the kids say. Wouldn't you?

Pause. She looks across at him.

You see.

Silence. She smiles.

And what you don't know – and now I'm going to be outrageous, even more arrogant than usual, what you have no idea about . . . Was I – am I – the future?

Al *is quiet, shaken, watching her.*

Elinor (*turns towards the music, shivers slightly*)   I wish they'd stop playing that horrible music though. (*She smokes.*) Termination music . . .

Al (*quiet, slowly*)   Elinor, you know the idea, my garbage proposal. (*He smiles.*) The Sun Garbage, do you remember?

Elinor Yes, it was a super idea.

Al I cannot make it come out. And I cannot create the circumstances where I feel I'm going to get there. I have abandoned it. (*He looks at her.*) We should have worked together. Imagine what we could have done! With my admin and your genius. (*Louder.*) Why did we never work together?

Elinor Because this was not the time.

Al What do you mean by that? If I'd asked you that day, when I had the chance, to form the unit with me, I *ought* to have asked you!

Elinor It would have made no difference. I'm very fond of you, Albie, (*Steely.*) but I would have never wanted to work with you, under any circumstances.

Pause.

Al Jesus, Elinor . . . (*Pause.*) even today . . . you're so implacable.

Elinor Yes. (*Pause. She watches him for a moment.*) Now find the hat.

Al (*nervous laugh*)   Of course. (*He moves among bags.*) It's got more difficult now!

Elinor   Maybe this is the way I can avoid the ceremony. (*She mimics.*) The old bastard intoning 'it is our great and long overdue pleasure to honour our colleague' and I'm NOT THERE! I'll get in my car and sail out of here, why not? (*She looks at* **Al**.) Perhaps we should, Albie, get in the old Morris and escape.

Al   Great idea.

Elinor   Yes it is. (*Suddenly with feeling.*) Oh, God, I wish I could!

Pause, the music changes.

That sounds ominous, doesn't it. (*Nervous laugh, moving along the bench. Suddenly she's very nervous, now it's so close.*) I was sitting here, on this very bench, on my first day in this building, still a schoolgirl, waiting for my interview. It'll be full of media students very soon. (*She laughs.*) It's very appropriate, everything I've spent my time filtering out of my life . . . coming here in a big hurry.

Al *picks up a bag from the centre of the stage. It contains an empty tin of baked beans. He rips it open.* **Elinor** *is upstage, smoking.*

Al (*very precise*)   Elinor died eighteen months later, in a way she would have approved of, might even have delighted her. She suddenly keeled over while shopping one day. She was carrying, tantalisingly, three boxes of A4 paper, as if she was preparing to set something down. She still worked on a 1950s Olivetti. But there was nothing typed yet. Without access to a lab – she hadn't quite finished.

He smiles.

Her handwritten notes were infuriatingly indecipherable, naturally. I *tried* but they were dense, spidery, secret. The builders have finished the renovation. But the building is standing empty, because of an inter-departmental row about finance. There is just silence here, of course, and the gradually fading smell of new paint in the passages.

Christopher *enters abruptly.*

Christopher   Come on, it's time. For Chrissake, what have you been doing in here? It's her entrance *now*. She's going to be late.

Al   Shit! Yes! But we haven't been able to find the hat.

Elinor   Doesn't matter, Albie. (*She laughs.*) My one anarchic gesture – to enter bareheaded!

Christopher   Give them a shock, good. I can't believe those faces in there. They're so predictable. They *are* all craning their necks to look at me. What does a disgraced scientist look like? It really *is* an ordeal – even worse than I thought. I'm terrified. After today I'm never coming back. But I had to be here for this, Elinor. (*To* **Al**.) You want to take her in?

Al   No, you take Elinor. That's how it should be.

Christopher   Or all three of us in a row? (*He smiles.*) Make a bigger splash!

Al   No. I'm quite happy. I'll be right behind. (*He grins.*) But don't say where I belong.

Elinor   No. We won't. Not today. (*Quite anxious to know the answer.*) Is it as good a turnout as Albie says?

Christopher   Better!

Al *helps straighten* **Elinor**'*s robes, as* **Elinor** *smiles.*

Al   We can whisper as we go down the aisle, to ease the tension.

Elinor   Whisper what?

Al   I don't know . . . about the weather. (*Softly.*) Or what your work really is! What a time to tell!

Elinor (*laughs*)   That's a good try, Albie, one of your very best.

Al (*suddenly*)   Shit! Where are the bells? Come on . . . come on! They should have started. At least then today will *seem* complete. (*Reaching for walkie-talkie.*) I may have to see to this —

But the bells start, just as he's about to go into action.

Ah, we made it!

Elinor   Good. I knew you would arrange it well, Albie.

Pause.

Christopher   Right! Everybody ready? One, two, three . . .

Christopher *exits.* **Al** *is about to, he turns.* **Elinor** *has not moved.*

Al (*impatient*)   Elinor? What are you doing? Come on.

Elinor   Patience. (*She takes a drag.*) I'm coming.

She looks across at him.

Fade.

Sweet Panic

Sweet Panic was first performed at the Hampstead Theatre, London, on 1 February 1996. The cast was as follows:

Clare	Harriet Walter
Mrs Trevel	Saskia Reeves
Martin	Mark Tandy
Richard	Rupert Penry-Jones
Gina	Kate Isitt
Mr Boulton	Philip Bird

Directed by Stephen Poliakoff
Designed by Tom Piper
Lighting by David Hersey
Sound by John A. Leonard

The time is the present.

Act One

Scene One

The set not cluttered, part a sense of a room, part a sense of the city. London. **Clare** *is in her late thirties. Alone on stage unrolling a chewing-gum packet. She takes out the chewing-gum but does not yet put it in her mouth. She looks up at us.*

Clare Leo is twelve. He comes to see me once a week. He is intelligent, always goes to school, always on time – but then does his best to ruin any class he's in. He specialises in singing obscene versions of television theme tunes.

She sits, stretches out her legs and stares at her shoes. Rather elegant shoes.

He's very proud of his sneakers. Which in fact aren't like any sneakers I've seen. Dyed a strange purple.

She starts chewing the gum, and becomes Leo. Conveying the essence of a feisty twelve-year-old without doing a totally direct impersonation.

(*As Leo.*) It's the worst that could happen. My mum and dad are taking me on holiday for a week. It's the worst because whatever happens they'll make out we had a really WICKED time – that's what they think I say when I'm pleased. They'll make out it was great . . . and *you* know what's going to happen . . . *you* know how it'll be.

She takes out the chewing-gum and sticks it carefully on some surface. Leo's father, **Mr Boulton,** *comes on and sits in a chair opposite her, a small table between them.*

Boulton It was good, it was fine . . . travelling through France without incident. We had a very good time, we survived.

Clare (*calmly*) Survived, or had a good time?

Boulton It was excellent . . . I hope it means the beginning of the end of Leo having to come here.

Clare   I don't think we've quite got to that yet.

Boulton   No? . . . No . . . As you will remember . . . the alternative to you . . . (*He stops*.)

Clare   What about the alternatives?

Boulton   Were not acceptable, family therapy, all that communal exposure . . . no, no. You see Leo on his own, that's fine. I'm sure we're moving towards success.

Clare (*gently*)   In time.

Boulton   I'm watching for changes, I think I can see signs.

He jangles coins in his pocket.

We had a *family* holiday, as you'll have heard. It was amazing, I kept on saying, so this is how it's done! Maybe I was a little preoccupied with my work . . . For the first forty-eight hours. You know my line of work . . . Ready Cooked Meals.

Clare   Ready Cooked Meals?

Boulton   Yes, we devise them for the major chains. I was awaiting news . . . a particular project, a new product.

Clare   What is the new product?

Boulton   A new instant meal, a return to the snack in a cup, you know, adding hot water, but a deluxe version. News of its progress is important to me – in fact I had to stop once or twice to phone as we were motoring along. But there was Leo, on the back seat sometimes singing along to the radio . . . enjoying the scenery. We even had a night of dancing! You know, Brits abroad . . . hair down, doing the conga (*He smiles*.) well, half a conga, the tail of a conga.

Suddenly he gets up.

I'm afraid I need to feed the meter, that's the trouble with these central London locations . . . excuse me . . . I know your time is precious, I'll be right back.

He exits.

Clare *walks over and takes the chewing-gum from where she carefully placed it and puts it back in her mouth.*

Clare (*as Leo*)   So – there we are travelling through France. I'm on the back seat and Dad – Dad is going on and on about his work, about whether they're going to OK it – how much he wants it to happen. We're eating all this fucking good food, I don't mind French food, some of my mates mind, but I don't, so we're eating this FANTASTIC food, and Dad doesn't even notice, he's just thinking about his Ready Cooked Meals!

One time we do play a game together, while we're going along . . . Dad's idea of a game, spot the English-made car with a French registration number! Not a great game – a little slow because there's only one every half an hour.

We stay a night in this sort of Holiday Inn, not a proper Holiday Inn.

And Mum insists – she really insists, on DANCING. My dad kind of 'walks' behind her. I'm sitting *watching*, of course. Jesus . . . you should have seen it! She looked so fat . . . gross . . . arms wobbling. No, I'm sorry, that's what she looked like.

Clare *chewing gum for a moment.*

And then in the car the next morning they begin quarrelling about whether they're on the right road. And Mum starts shouting and shrieking, 'I'm map reading – you NEVER believe me about anything, you always think I've got it wrong.' And it's like I'm invisible, on the back seat, like they've completely forgotten there's anybody else in the car. And then Mum, she's shrieking, she reaches down, I promise you and she opens the passenger door while we're going along at sixty miles an hour – she does, only a few inches, but she does. Screaming brakes, emergency stop! Nyeeaaaar, (*Mimics noise.*) yell, yell, yell at each other.

And suddenly it's 'Ssshhh, Leo's there, he's listening' – and then there are these two anxious faces looking at me, my

MUM and DAD, you know blinking at me – like, 'you didn't actually hear anything, did you, Leo?'

Clare *removes the chewing-gum.* **Boulton** *enters. He stands across the stage in a sharp hurried mood, clanking the change in his pocket.*

Boulton   Right, actually . . . change of plan. I think I'd better move, there's a clamping van on the prowl and a traffic warden standing just where I've parked so feeding the meter's not possible. I've two minutes left – still . . . on the meter.

Clare   You're right, parking has become a nightmare in the centre of town.

Boulton   So. We've kept abreast of things, know where we are.

He moves to go.

I have the bank holiday with Leo, now. My wife and I, three whole days to fill, what a prospect! (*Slight nervous laugh.*)

Clare *opens her mouth to speak. He holds up his hand.*

Boulton   No, please, it'll be fine. We'll keep him occupied. No chance to misbehave.

(*At exit.*) Have a good holiday, it's almost the real beginning of summer, isn't it, the first May bank holiday. (*He exits.*)

Gina *enters, a young woman of twenty-two, she is holding an object wrapped up in plastic bags and tied tightly with string.*

Clare   That's all?

Gina   That's all – that was the last appointment – I mean, he was really an extra too, it was meant to be just a ten-minute chat.

Clare   Yes, but I let him, because it was the end of the day. (*She smiles.*) Finally his meter ran out . . . ! But now we're through.

Gina   Except –

Clare   Except what?

Gina   Jess came back.

Clare   She came back? (*Very interested.*) She's not here now?

Gina   No. She came all the way back to give you this.

Gina *puts down the plastic bag.*

Clare   Yes I wondered what that was.

Gina *moves to the exit.*

Gina   Oh, and Mrs Trevel phoned.

Clare   Again? I've already spoken to her *twice* today.

Gina (*at exit*)   She said it was pretty urgent . . . She's going to ring again, should be about now.

She exits.

Clare *is examining with curiosity the plastic bag. She begins to undo the string and take away the layers of plastic, because the parcel is bundled like a surprise package.*

Clare   Jess – a thirteen-year-old girl.

She takes away another layer of the parcel's wrapping.

Jess has been referred to me for over a year. On the NHS. Lives with her mother's new boyfriend in north London. She will hardly attend school at all. Checks in, for half an hour, and then she's off. Instead she moves around the city on her own very particular walks, and things happen to her.

She lights a cigarette.

But she is always on time for me.

She stands near the parcel and becomes Jess, again conveying her essence rather than impersonating a child.

Tell you about an interesting walk, to the video shop. We're in the flat, Fernando, that's my mum's boyfriend, he's as English as me but he likes to be called Fernando. We've been watching some bonking movies, lots of buttocks, a whole afternoon of buttocks. Fernando likes to throw mashed potato at the screen – it's quite good actually, the cold mashed potato sticks to the screen, and the buttocks move up and down through it. Also, there's a movie, somebody's head being bitten off, while he's having sex . . . ugly bastard, it was definitely an improvement without the head!

So I go to the video shop and I choose a movie for him. I know what he likes, by now . . . obviously! And the girl behind the counter she's all pale, and like, when I say, 'Can I have this please?' she ignores me . . . so I ask again, very polite, very nice, and she bursts into tears! And I say, 'What the fuck's the matter?' and she says, 'We're all a bit sensitive at the moment because we were ROBBED yesterday.' Armed robbery, firearms, people being tied up, the whole lot. And then she looks at my video and says, 'Oh no no no you can't have that, it's the wrong certificate, you're too young to see that, it's too violent!' (*She smiles.*) Yeah . . . I thought you'd be interested in that . . .

Martin *enters, a man of forty.*

Martin   I can't believe it – you've finished! (*He smiles.*) Only overrun by thirty minutes.

Clare   Yes. I've almost finished.

Martin (*putting his arms around her*)   Ready for the off – into deepest Norfolk! Beat the traffic, I have a special route of shortcuts worked out (*He grins.*) as you'd expect. And what's more for the whole three days, I have a holiday schedule – hour by hour.

Clare   A schedule? (*She kisses him.*) Oh, I love your schedules – in small doses! I'll give myself over utterly to this one, I think. No responsibility for any plans.

Martin   It's all play and no work, graded in a curve that gets lazier and lazier. I'm not even taking my manuscript, no proofreading. And I bought provisions, including, magically, some samphire. Taking samphire to Norfolk – a more stylish coals to Newcastle!

Clare *returning to Jess's package.*

Clare   Samphire – it's that green stringy stuff, isn't it?

Martin The East Anglian asparagus — we will sit down and guzzle as soon as we get there, hot melted butter dripping all over the place. (*He touches her.*) And you'll be able to leave all the kids behind, all their worries.

Watching what **Clare** *is doing, unwrapping the package.*

And any strange parcels will be left behind as well. What is that?

Clare It's from one of the kids (*She undoes the last part of the wrapping.*) and you won't easily guess what this is. Nor will I. Though I have a general idea.

She reveals what's under all the wrapping. A model, out of cardboard, of the Albert Memorial, covered in its scaffolding. It is a crude but vivid representation.

Martin Jesus — the Albert Memorial! (*He smiles.*) That would have taken some guessing.

Clare She walks around London, this girl — and she started doing these cardboard models, about the things she sees.

She brings them to me — to get a reaction. We have this poker game — she knows I'm going to be boring, clinical, 'why have you made it look like this? What are you trying to show me, Jess?', pushing hard to find what 'statement' she's making. And she's thinking 'why doesn't she just tell me it's fucking good?'

They can be quite unexpected in fact — there's usually something hidden inside.

She lifts the outer part, the scaffolding, off. She then lifts the top of the Memorial off, and then recoils having pricked herself on something.

Shit! what is that?

Martin (*peering into Albert Memorial*) Yes, what is it? I think it's meant to be a giant hypodermic needle.

Clare (*laughs*) That's just like her!

Martin She got hold of a big spike from somewhere.

Clare   She gets these ideas – what's growing underneath all those covers on the Albert Memorial?

Martin   I should meet her.

Gina *enters*.

Gina   I'm afraid . . . I'm sorry, I didn't mean to let her up – I didn't know what to do (*Slight pause*.) but Mrs Trevel is here.

Clare   What, right now – here?

Gina   Yes. She says it won't take a moment. But it is important. She just wants to ask you one thing.

Clare (*moving*)   I know what she wants to ask me.

Martin (*to* **Clare**)   Say you've gone already. (*To* **Gina**.) Say she's gone.

Clare   No. I don't like to do that. I better see her. (*To* **Gina**.) *For a moment*.

Gina *exits*.

Clare   Sorry about this. I've already spoken to her twice today.

Martin (*smiles*)   You work too hard – did I ever tell you that? It's a gorgeous day out there . . . and we've got to beat the rush hour.

Clare (*moving the model*)   There's something about this time of the year, just before summer starts, when all the parents seem to want to come in and consult. I won't let her stay.

Mrs Trevel *enters as* **Clare** *is saying this. She's in her late thirties, same age as* **Clare**.

Mrs Trevel   I'm terribly sorry about this. You can see me, can't you? I know this is wrong, just turning up, I shouldn't be causing an extra appointment . . .

Clare   It's fine, Mrs Trevel.

Martin *looks at her, smiles and exits*.

Clare   I'm about to leave the office. So this will have to
be —

Mrs Trevel (*cutting her off*)   I understand. Absolutely.

She sits opposite **Clare**.

This will be the briefest interview. Right. (*Slight pause.*) Deep
breath . . . (*Another slight pause.*) I know I've gone on and on
about this . . . we've spoken on the phone . . .

Pause. She looks directly at **Clare**.

BUT SHOULD GEORGE GO AWAY? . . . Tomorrow?
. . . On his own?

Clare   Mrs Trevel, we *have* gone over this, at length.

Mrs Trevel   Already. Yes. It's just his first trip away, since
all the trouble started, I mean, him curling up in bed, head to
the wall, refusing to go to school, and everything.

And now going all the way to Gloucestershire, Upper
Slaughter, that ridiculous name for a village, I mean, I know
it doesn't seem far, but —

Clare   Mrs Trevel . . . we both know I've said this before —
I cannot advise you. That is not how I work. Or how this
decision should be made. It is between you and your
husband, and George —

Mrs Trevel   To work it out.

Clare   Yes, to work it out. Does George still want to go?

Mrs Trevel   Yes, I don't know how passionately, but he
does.

Clare   So we know that. We know it's tomorrow, and what
it might mean to him if it was cancelled, suddenly, after he's
been thinking about it for several weeks. And now what is
being weighed against that? What are the concerns that
count against that, Mrs Trevel?

Mrs Trevel   Very judicial. A summing up. Quite right.
We're weighing — I'm weighing — against, the fact that this is
a very formidable family, he's going to stay with, the Olivier-

Jones's. The father's a very senior civil servant, the boy, the son who's invited George, is incredibly good at everything, and I mean everything, top at French, top at maths, even absurd things like archery. The house they have is huge . . . it all may be intimidating, reminding George how far he is behind.

Pause.

I feel – I just feel . . . (*She pauses.*)

Clare Yes?

Mrs Trevel I JUST FEEL . . . (*She pauses.*) the elements, you know, the elements, you know . . . it's delicate. (*She looks up.*) And you spend all this time with George, you know George, you've been looking at what's been going on inside . . .

Clare Yes, (*Patiently.*) Mrs Trevel, if I may say so, it's not helpful, to think of George as being behind . . .

Mrs Trevel Yes. You're right. What a fusspot I must appear! I hate to seem a whining mother, and I know my time is up – it is up, isn't it? – but can I ask you one direct question?

Clare Of course. (*She smiles.*) It'll depend on what it is if you get a direct answer.

Mrs Trevel Would you tell me – if you thought it was *wrong* for George to go? If you knew it was wrong, would you say?

Clare Mrs Trevel, I know this seems a predictable answer, a frustrating answer, but it really has to be something George and you talk through.

Mrs Trevel But if you knew it was wrong?

Clare If I thought there were obvious factors that –

Mrs Trevel So you think he should go? Tell me please – I know I said one question, but tell me.

Clare (*trying to remain patient*) Unless there's anything new that's occurred which I'm unaware of –

Mrs Trevel On balance? He should go? . . . On balance?

Clare Yes.

Mrs Trevel Yes?

Clare But it –

Mrs Trevel But it's between me and George. Yes, yes.

Silence.

Clare (*moving at the desk trying to suggest the interview is over*) So . . .

Mrs Trevel So – good. Thanks.

But she doesn't move.

There's just one other thing, I know you need to be off. The whole city's about to migrate, isn't it. (*She looks at her watch and laughs.*) There, I've looked at the time for you!
I just wondered, you are going out of town for the holiday weekend, are you?

Slight pause. **Clare** *watching her.*

Clare Yes.

Mrs Trevel I have the office number here, and I have your London home number – you were kind enough . . . I don't know if you have two lines there, but I have your number.

She looks at **Clare**.

But is it possible to have your mobile number?

A momentary pause.

Clare I don't have a mobile.

Mrs Trevel Really?

Clare I have no need. I'm usually here, or at home.

Mrs Trevel Of course. It's just – I'm sure it won't arise, but I would feel – it would be nice – if there was some way of reaching you. If there were problems with George, if I could get in touch.

Clare   I will be checking my number at home regularly. And here.

Mrs Trevel   Of course, if you haven't a mobile, that is the next best thing, obviously. You'll be checking often? Good. (*She looks around.*) I realise all the things you've got to do. I know I'm very fortunate, to be given this time, unscheduled, I'm grateful. I'll leave as quickly as I came in. (*She smiles.*) I can try. Hopefully do no more damage to your weekend. So – I've gone.

She exits. **Clare** *alone on stage.*

Clare   Jesus! (*She moves.*) JESUS! Sometimes . . .

Martin *enters.*

Clare   Sometimes one really wants – (*Lightly.*) to say JUST SHUT UP.

Martin   Absolutely, you should try it.

Clare (*she laughs*)   Oh yeah? And poor George, he's a quiet very watchful child. Big eyes staring at you. Takes his time. Hardly a child in torment. He really wants to go away and stay with his friend.
He's always finding money on the pavement, his speciality. Presents you very carefully with his own pile of coins. (*She moves.*) Certain parents find it very difficult to realise some children just take a pause in their development, to look around, to take the temperature of the next stage. And that's OK.

Martin   I don't know how you stop yourself screaming at mothers like that – (*He mimics.*) Don't you realise it's you that's the fucking problem!

Clare   Yes, well, Mrs Trevel, is the sort, unfortunately, who is horrified at the very suggestion that she should talk to someone. Actually she's usually not quite as persistent as this – (*She moves.*) It was only today . . . it was a little extreme.

She turns abruptly.

She wanted the number of my mobile, you know.

Martin   Oh, Christ! You didn't give it to her, did you?

Clare   No. (*She moves.*) I'm only away three days – and she wants the mobile!

Martin   What a nightmare that would be – her popping up while we're having a bath . . . or at three in the morning.

Clare   But she'll still be calling the home number, she was already getting in the mood for it. 'Is it all right for George to go to bed so late?' A whole barrage, expecting a quick response.

Martin   Leave the machine off. So she can't leave a message.

Clare   No, that wouldn't be a good idea.

Martin   Why not? All your possible urgent cases, the real ones, have the mobile number, don't they?

Clare   Yes. (*She moves.*) I'll think about it . . .
She'll just call here anyway, (*Smiles.*) swamp the machine here.

Martin   But it's perfectly possible to say you don't constantly check the office number at the weekend – because you don't.

Clare (*lightly*)   I don't know, it's getting very complicated, Martin.

Martin   No, it isn't. (*Lightly.*) It's making sure you're not a slave to modern communications. And more important, it's establishing a zone – free of Mrs Trevel!

Blackout.

Scene Two

Clare *walks on, lights a cigarette.*

Clare   Jess — on the news.

She becomes Jess.

I don't know why they don't have *music* while they read the news on TV. It really sounds EMPTY because they don't have music — ALL THE WAY THROUGH. Not yet. I'm going to write and suggest it — because they'd get a lot more people watching.

You know the weathermen, when they do the weather they change the weather, the maps, by stepping on a pedal on the floor, they do, I read about it!

So I've had this idea, the news, while they're doing it, they can sit with these pedals under their desk and when there's a really sad item, some people dying in a war, they can play the sad pedal — and when there's something a bit better, they can give us the trumpet pedal . . . you know, they can work it like an organ! Their little feet tapping away! NEWS WITH MUSIC!

She moves.

The other thing about the news is, everybody that comes on, absolutely every time, they always say, 'But, at the end of the day . . .' doesn't matter if it's about politics or fish fingers, out it comes — 'But, *at the end of the day* —' like everything makes sense now. Wow! But, at the end of the fucking day, they have, in fact, not said a fucking thing!

Clare *sits, starts chewing gum.*

And Leo, on the news.

She becomes Leo.

The news on television is real — a lot of the time. But sometimes when there isn't enough, they make it up.

They have a special room, where there's this one man, only one, who *thinks it up.* So when they don't have enough, they

send for him, and he says, 'What sort of thing do you want?'
And they tell him. And then he invents it.

He does! And he gets paid really well. Only works three days
a week. Good job, that!

She exits.

Empty stage, we hear the tape-machine, **Mrs Trevel***'s voice loud,
coming over main auditorium speakers.*

Mrs Trevel   Could you call me . . . this is Caroline Trevel,
George's mother, as soon as you get this message, please.
There's no answer from your home phone number. Please.

Gina *enters, morning light, she stands by answering machine, rewinds
the tape a little, and then stands very still listening to it.*

The second message comes out of answering machine on stage: **Mrs
Trevel***'s voice, very urgent.*

Mrs Trevel   I'm now here . . . on a train . . . please ring
the following number (*She gives a Gloucestershire number.*) . . .
that's where I'm heading as soon as you get this message,
there's still no answer from your home.

The message clicks off. Then there's a really loud, imploring voice.

RING ME. PLEASE. RING ME.

Gina *stands for a moment staring down at the tape machine.* **Clare**
enters. **Gina** *startled.*

Clare   You're here very early, Gina.

Gina   Yes. I woke at five thirty this morning, for some
reason. And I had a few things to do in town – so here I am.

Clare   I usually beat you to it – (*She laughs.*) I'll have to
start getting in earlier! Did you have a good weekend?
Manage to wind down? Do anything exciting?

Gina   It was fine. It was very satisfactory.

Clare   Very satisfactory! (*Laughs.*) You're always so
cryptic, Gina – come on – that could cover a thousand sins!

Gina (*coolly*)   I did a couple of tasks I've been putting off doing. It was OK. Things worked out.

Clare *realises she is not going to get any more.*

Gina   I was listening to the messages – they're all from Mrs Trevel.

Clare   Yes, well, I was rather expecting that. I had a weekend largely free from calls. I somehow managed it. It's usually pretty difficult for me to have a real break. I keep wondering about various cases –

Gina   But not Mrs Trevel.

Clare   No.

Gina (*crisply*)   I'll make some coffee. (*As she exits.*) I think there are eight calls on there in all.

Clare   Eight!

She presses the machine.

Mrs Trevel   You *must* ring me – it is absolutely essential you ring me.

Gina *enters.* **Clare** *doesn't look up, she is suddenly preoccupied.*

Clare   On any of these calls – does she say if anything's happened?

Gina   Mrs Trevel is here.

Clare (*startled*)   She's here? Now?

Gina   Yes. She's just come in. She says she'd like to talk to you. (*Slight pause.*) If she could.

Clare (*impatient with* **Gina**'s *contained manner*)   Well, show her in . . . !

She pauses for a moment, straightening herself.

Mrs Trevel *enters.*

Mrs Trevel   There you are . . .

She stops.

First of all, to get one thing clear, you *are* agreeing to see me?

Clare   Of course. Of course I'm agreeing. I hope everything's well . . . with George, and −

Mrs Trevel   Why didn't you return any of my calls?

Clare   I just got your messages now. I was literally listening to them, this very moment, I only got back this morning −

Mrs Trevel   I tried, goodness knows how many times − I left messages here, again and again. And there was no answer − never any answer from your home number.

Clare   I've explained, I've only just got in −

Mrs Trevel   Didn't you check your messages here − for heaven's sake? Didn't you hear me asking for you?

Momentary pause.

Clare   Has something happened, Mrs Trevel? Has something happened to George?

Mrs Trevel   I will be coming to that.
I just couldn't believe, after the discussion we had, just before the weekend. I could not *believe* I got no reply −

Clare   What has happened to George?

Mrs Trevel   Didn't you see the news? On the television? What were you doing all the time − didn't you see a single bulletin?

Clare   No. I didn't happen to watch any television.

Mrs Trevel   Or the radio, you didn't catch the radio − you were too busy for THAT EVEN.

Clare *trying to remain calm.*

Clare   Mrs Trevel, just tell me what's taken place? Where is George?

Silence.

Mrs Trevel's *head bends for a moment.*

Clare   Are you all right?

Mrs Trevel   HE RAN AWAY.

Clare   What? Where to? He's been found, hasn't he?

Mrs Trevel   It was on the *news* bulletins – child of eleven *missing*. Seeing it on the national news, George's picture . . . they asked for a photograph, George's face staring back out of the television – you can't imagine the shock, seeing that.

Clare   Mrs Trevel, has he been *found*?

Mrs Trevel   There were helicopters, police dogs, police radios buzzing all the time.
AFTER TWO DAYS, AFTER NEARLY TWO DAYS, THEY FOUND HIM . . .
You can't believe how long that seemed . . . that's when I so wanted you, to be able to speak.

Clare   It must have been incredibly worrying. Please just tell me – if you can, what happened? Where did they find him . . . ? (*Quiet.*) Where is he now?

Mrs Trevel (*suddenly*)   Of course he's *alive*. Otherwise I wouldn't be here. He's safe now.

Clare   Thank God for that. (*Quiet.*) I'd assumed he was 'all right', but . . . what a terrible thing to have to go through. (*Momentary pause.*) Do you think you could tell me the sequence of events, when you're ready, how it happened?

Slight pause.

Mrs Trevel   I don't know how you missed the news. I really don't. It wasn't on every bulletin – but even so, how on earth did you miss it?

Clare   With respect, I don't think that's what's important now . . . It would really help me to hear the complete facts, as soon as that's possible – and of course I must see George. Where was he found?

Slight pause.

Mrs Trevel   At the bottom of the garden.

Clare (*startled*)   What do you mean?

Mrs Trevel There's a clump of trees, a wood, at the Olivier-Jones's, a rather horrible wood at the bottom of the garden. He was there, he'd built this sort of hide – out of logs and dead branches, and other things . . . He was there, at the bottom of the garden.

Clare Oh, I see – . . . so it was like he decided, possibly as a dare, to spend a night in the woods . . . It was like camping –

Mrs Trevel It wasn't camping. It was NOT camping. Are you suggesting we didn't look hard enough?

Clare No, of course not. Any child that doesn't want to be found for two days – that evades the police and all that – obviously something is going on there that we must –

Mrs Trevel (*cutting her off*) You think he just went off for an adventure . . . in the woods and *I* blew it all up into something enormous. Is that what you think?

Clare *No*. Again, of course not. I was just making the point, rather unnecessarily, that he didn't 'Run Away', in the sense of running off to the city, or hitching along the motorway. This is something different . . .

Mrs Trevel I can't *believe* you said that . . . That he went *camping*.

Clare Please, let's not get stuck on this. It really is not what matters. When can I see George? The sooner the better, obviously.

Mrs Trevel You won't be seeing George again.

Slight pause.

Clare (*startled*) Really? You mean he won't be coming to any more sessions?

Mrs Trevel What else could I have meant? It's best to be blunt, isn't it?

Clare I understand you being upset, of course, and angry about what's occurred. It's natural –

Mrs Trevel　You needn't worry about George. He's just not coming here any more.

Very slight pause.

Clare　If that continues to be the situation, Mrs Trevel, then I can give you the name of a colleague, because it's very important somebody talks to George.

Mrs Trevel　You really don't need to concern yourself with any of that. George is nothing to do with you now.

Clare　No. Mrs Trevel.
I do have to insist that I have contact with whoever is going to see George, so I can liaise with them –

Mrs Trevel (*suddenly*)　*Why* was there no answer from your home number? – From your home answer machine? Why did it just ring and ring?

Clare　I realise it must have been very maddening, not to be able to contact me. But I have to say it is very unlikely I would have been able to do any more than the police – who were on the spot.

Mrs Trevel　Yes. Naturally you would say that, wouldn't you. *So* – did I miss your explanation? Or didn't you give me one?

Momentary pause.

Clare　I will answer all your questions, about phones, if you like, in due course – but I think we've *got* to get George's arrangements clear.

Mrs Trevel　Was the answering machine faulty, or had it been left off?

Clare (*very slight pause*)　I believe it was left off – I was in a great rush getting away, as you may remember.

Mrs Trevel *takes out notebook, and starts writing.*

Mrs Trevel　I'm just making a note of that. You don't mind, if I make a note? (*As she writes.*) And of course, no

checks were made on your machine here. At the office.
Where all my messages were waiting for you?

Clare   It *was* a holiday, I was trying to have a genuine
break. Now . . .

Mrs Trevel   A 'genuine break' . . . (*She notes this down.*) Of
course.

She closes notebook.

I'm running out of time for this interview. I have things to
do. I was here on a reconnaissance −

Clare   A reconnaissance?

Mrs Trevel   Yes, I think that's the right word. I wanted to
hear your explanation.

She holds notebook tightly.

Which I now possess. You must forgive me if I've been rude
. . . Maybe I haven't been rude. (*She looks at* **Clare**.) You
don't have children, do you?

Clare   No . . .

Mrs Trevel *gets up.*

Mrs Trevel   I have no idea, at this precise moment, where
this reconnaissance is going to lead. Whether there's going to
be a second stage − or not. I just know you're not going to see
George again.

Clare   I would urge you −

Mrs Trevel   FORGET GEORGE.

She moves.

What should interest you far more, is whether you'll see *me*
again . . .
Or whether you'll be totally free of me.

She moves off.

I expect we've cleared things up . . .
I just have to consider the position . . . What do you think?

She exits.

Clare *alone for a second. She is startled by the encounter, but begins to recover her cool.* **Gina** *enters with coffee.*

Clare You're a bit late with the coffee, Gina. (*She smiles.*) Might have helped break the atmosphere a bit, if you'd come in while *she* was still here.

Gina I'm sorry. I couldn't find the tin.

Clare Mrs Trevel was quite upset, understandably. I will need to dictate a long letter to her *today*.

She looks searchingly at **Gina**.

Did you see anything on the television, about George, did you catch any of it?

Gina No, I didn't see it.

Clare (*sharp*) But you *know* what I'm talking about – you know what happened to George?

Gina Yes. I do now. I *just* saw a little story, on the inside page of the newspaper . . . right this very moment, only a few lines, with 'Boy Found' . . . and George's name.

Clare Yes. (*Smiles, relieved.*) I *thought*, if you'd known Gina, you would have warned me . . . before she arrived.

Pause.

Gina (*walking up to her*) There's a list of your appointments for today. And there's somebody waiting to see you.

Clare Who?

Gina It's a surprise. *He* wants it to be a surprise. He says you'll know him.

Clare OK. A very *brief* surprise, please, Gina.

Gina *exits.*

Clare In fact I'm not exactly in the mood for surprises this morning.

Richard *enters. He is nineteen years old – a beautiful tall boy.*

Clare *doesn't recognise him.*

Clare   Hello? Yes?

Gina   This is —

Richard   No. Don't say my name! Please!

He stares across at **Clare**.

Hello, Miss Attwood.

Clare   I'm sorry. You'll have to help me. We know each
other, right?
But at the moment — I can't quite picture . . .

Richard   I'll give you a clue — five and a half years ago . . .
I sat here, opposite you.

Richard *grins*.

Clare   Well, I guessed *that*. But (*She's staring at him.*) I'm still
not quite —

Richard (*charming smile*)   And — I was wearing, the last
time I was here with you, I was wearing a shirt with huge
mock ink stains all over it . . . Remember? Pretend blotches.

Clare   Richard! Of course. Richard Mellinger! Jesus, for a
moment I just couldn't . . . you're so tall now! Such a big lad!

Richard   I grew a little. Yes. (*He grins*.) So people say. Five
years is nothing for you — but for me . . . !

Clare   Where have you been, what you been up to?

Richard   It's been great, I've been in America. On a
foundation course.

To **Gina** *who has been watching with interest.*

Can I just have a moment? Alone with Miss Attwood?

Gina *exits.* **Richard** *turns back to* **Clare**.

Richard   I promise it'll *only* be a moment.

Clare   You look really well. I can't believe it's you . . .
tanned . . . relaxed . . .

Richard   Yes. (*He grins.*) I could feel you scanning me.
(*Teasing.*) Feel that gaze panning across me – got to about
here now, haven't you? (*He laughs, indicating his elbow.*)
Noticing things, picking up clues . . . ?

Clare   No!

Richard (*grins*)   Oh yes. Beaming in on anything, my wrist
watch, or whether I'm looking you straight in the eyes!

Clare (*laughs*)   I'm not on duty, yet.

Richard   I want to tell you all about it. About me. Not
now, I realise!
I brought this for you . . .

He gives **Clare** *a present.*

It's just the smallest thing, not a serious gift.

Clare *opens it, it's a large elaborate black necklace.*

Clare   How exotic, Richard. (*Warm smile.*) It's great,
lovely.

Richard   Thought you could wear it when you were
dancing, you know swing it around, as you bop.

Clare (*laughs*)   And clear the floor, probably! Decapitate a
few people . . .

Richard   I know I mustn't take up time, I want to make an
appointment so I can see you properly.
I expect a drink is out of the question – me taking you out for
a drink?

Clare   An appointment would be better.

Richard   Right. I'll keep everything for then, because now
you've got the whole day ahead of you – full of spotty kids,
rabbiting on about Mum and Dad, how they hate the
dentist, how they're being beaten up at school – they're
probably even worse than I was.

Clare (*smiles*)   And look at you now! Yes, I'd love to hear
everything, Richard.

Richard   Right. Good.

Clare (*warmly*)   I'm still working out . . . if I *was* staring it's because I'm still looking for where that little boy is, in that face, the little boy that used to sulk in the corner.

Richard (*charming smile*)   Well, look hard. It *is* me.

Clare   I like your clothes, Richard. That's a wonderful jacket – and –

Richard   And Italian shoes – that's right!

Clare   Very cosmopolitan.

Richard   Yeah, that's the word! (*He grins.*) I'm working hard at it anyway, to be cosmopolitan. I think it's a great thing to be.

He moves.

And I've been away so much . . . just walking around town these last few days, London has CHANGED.
I mean, I'm amazed at the difference, whole clusters of buildings have shot up – looking like they don't belong here at all.

He moves up to her.

I'm off. I just wanted to surprise you –

Clare   And you did.

Richard   When I see you properly – I'll tell you things, to make you laugh. My exploits, adventures, *and* my qualifications. Hope to impress you.

Clare (*gently*)   You don't need to impress me, Richard.

Richard   I'm going to leave it like that . . . tantalising . . . OK?

Richard *kisses her on the cheek, and leaves.*

Gina *enters.*

Gina   Who was *that*? He was gorgeous!

Clare   Wasn't he just . . . (*She smiles.*)
I never heard you so enthusiastic about anything, Gina.

Gina *watching her.*

Clare   Sometimes they sprout like that, transform . . .
become confident. And it's great to see.

Blackout.

Scene Two – A

Clare *enters wheeling a large flat trolley, on it a large flat object covered in plastic.*

Clare   Jess, after her success with the Albert Memorial –
managing to surprise me, not to mention drawing blood
(*Looks at her hand.*) – was definitely a success in her eyes.
So – she's announced she's now embarked on her own *series* of
models – the landmarks of London.

She lights cigarette, and moves trolley forward.

(*As Jess.*) OK – first up, I've done Harrods for you.

She surveys the big bundle on the trolley.

Before you look at it, and knowing how keen you are in seeing
'statements' in whatever I show you, I think a word of
explanation is in order.

And the explanation is – to take you on a bit of a walk. You
know how good I am on walks!

This is a shoplifting walk . . . right here, in the room. Yeah –
I thought that would get a reaction out of you.

The thing about nicking things in those stores – and it is so
obvious I don't know why many people don't do it – the
answer to the problem is, to EAT THE EVIDENCE. Yeah –
eat it all.
To go around nicking food and eat it before you leave the
fucking place. What they going to do – pump out your
stomach?
Here it is.

*She reveals large vivid cardboard model of Harrods, covered in
Japanese flags.*

So you're going through the Food Hall, OK, are you with
me? Marble everywhere you look – and the tourists are there,
shuffle, shuffle, very slow – and the people who *live* round
there are pushing through very fast, 'Excuse me, can I get by,
EXCUSE ME.'
What they really mean – is – 'Out of the way you fucking
foreign gits, wish you weren't in our city – but we need you
. . . so – excuse me.'

And in the middle of all that, I'm taking a king prawn here, a
chocolate truffle there – it's great, you should try it – and
above all CRYSTALLISED FRUIT, the easiest thing to
nick in the world, because of the handy round boxes.
And I'm shovelling them down me as fast as I can get hold of
them. Tastes disgusting after a bit of course.

So – you got that?

Now, look, (*Indicates model.*) Harrods, very recognisable I
think you will agree.
The Japanese flags are there, because I think that will be the
worst thing any of *them* could imagine – if the JAPANESE
bought Harrods. *And* –

She takes the Harrods dome off the model.

The top comes away and coming out of it is –

Out of the dome sticks a large plastic object covered in gunge.

This is meant to be part of a giant sneaker. A SNEAKER –
yes – is that me? Does that 'represent' me? I don't know, you
tell me.

And it is coated – as you can see and this is the good bit – with
CRYSTALLISED FRUIT. These are the actual things!
The whole dome – oozing crystallised fruit, like there's so
much in there, it's just got to *get out*!

What d'you think? That's Harrods! I hope when you next see
the real thing, it'll look exactly like that to you. – Yeah.

I want to make you look at all of London different – before
I've finished with you.

Scene Three

*Large model, in Jess's distinctive style is carried on upstage. It is much
the largest one yet.*

*It is a section of the white Nash terraces that overlook Regent's Park –
the roof/cupola raised on the central house – and out of its top is
sprouting a mass of spiky, futuristic aerials and satellite dishes, like a
great tangle of wire hair.*

*Music, as if from a bandstand, is drifting across the park, there's also a
picturesque environmentally conscious rubbish bin in the shape of a
wooden squirrel.*

Clare *is lying in the middle of the stage, on her front, sunbathing. She
is scantily clad, barefoot, the straps of her dress partially pulled down,
so she's lying barebacked. She's talking on her mobile phone, as she lies
on her front.*

Clare   *Come on*, I'm famished.

Where are you? At the top of Baker Street! Well, HURRY
UP. There's a band playing here and everything, it's perfect
picnic weather . . . and you're still lumbering up Baker
Street!

You know where I am? . . . What d'you mean between the
Nash terraces and the water? – That could almost mean any
part of the park! . . . Yes . . . near THAT tree . . .

No, I'm not . . . I'm stretched out – I was in a real erotic
reverie – and I'm going back to it . . .
(*She laughs.*) Who says it was about you! . . . I *thought* that
might make you walk faster! . . .

*She rings off, puts mobile phone away in her bag and lies down flat on
her stomach.*

For a second **Clare** *is alone with the music.*

Mrs Trevel *enters. She is wearing dark clothes. She is very bundled up for such a hot day. For a moment she leans against the rubbish bin, watching* **Clare**.

Clare *turns her head truly startled. For a moment she is at an incredible disadvantage. She sits up pulling up the straps of her dress trying to maintain her dignity.*

Clare   Mrs Trevel . . . !

Mrs Trevel   I thought it was you.

Clare   Heavens – what a surprise!

Mrs Trevel   It is – isn't it.

Clare   I was just taking my lunch hour . . . I very rarely do this . . . especially *here*. I work so close to the park – and yet I hardly ever use it, but today because it was so *hot* . . . (*Glancing at* **Mrs Trevel**.) It seemed a good idea.

Mrs Trevel   You really don't have to explain yourself to me. You're lying in the park, in your lunch hour – what could possibly be wrong with that?

Leaning against the litter bin, she takes out a cigarette.

I'm sure the park is full of other professionals, right at this moment – head teachers sunning themselves . . . topless hospital administrators . . . civil servants in bathing trunks, . . . maybe even a partially nude senior policewoman . . . Letting all the stress go. (*She smokes.*) Why not?

Clare (*lightly*)   Slightest sign of the sun and the British go mad, don't they nowadays. We rush out, tearing off all our clothes.

Pause. They look at each other. **Mrs Trevel** *glances at all the clothes she's wearing.*

Mrs Trevel   All except me, it appears. (*She blows smoke, smiles, relaxed.*) I'm sure the wheels are going round now . . . 'Why is she bundled up . . . is it because of some deep fundamental problem? . . . A complex about her body?'

Clare   Please, I didn't mean –

Mrs Trevel (*breezily*)   No, of course not.

She laughs.

I'd really confuse things now, wouldn't I, if I took my shoes off . . . started losing layers . . . !

She smokes.

Don't worry about it, no offence taken. I startled you after all.

And I know you're wondering two things.

Did I see your mobile phone?

And – am I here by complete accident? A bizarre coincidence.

Slight pause. She smiles.

Or am I in fact stalking you?

Clare   Stalking me! (*Startled laugh.*) That's very American. I thought that normally happened to famous film actresses, why would you want to do that?

Mrs Trevel   So you believe in coincidences then?

Clare   It depends, obviously, on the circumstances. In regard to this one – right now – I haven't made up my mind.

Mrs Trevel   Yes, well, it would be a rather surprising turn of events, if I was following you all over London, I agree. (*Pause, she laughs.*) I mean, that would be a wonderfully strange thing to happen.

The mobile phone rings faintly from inside **Clare**'s *bag.* **Clare** *glances up at* **Mrs Trevel**.

Mrs Trevel   Answer it, please, answer it.

Clare (*already taking phone out of bag. Into phone*)   Where are you? . . . Only there! . . . you're making very stately progress . . . (*Quiet, confidential.*) It would be a good idea, to hurry up. If you can.

She puts the phone away calmly.

It belongs to my partner – the phone. Recently acquired. He was phoning from a few streets away. He's just about to enter the park – I hope, with the *food*.

Mrs Trevel   You're having a picnic together? Matching lunch-hours, that's very well co-ordinated.

Clare   So how is *George*?

Mrs Trevel   He is absolutely fine.

Clare   And do we know any more about what happened?

Mrs Trevel   It all took place when you were away, on holiday. Don't worry about it.

Clare   And forgive me pursuing this point, have you arranged for him to see somebody else? I left several messages for you, you didn't call me back.

Slight pause.

Mrs Trevel   I think I'm going to really shock you, Miss Attwood. But I'm not interested in why George ran away.

Clare (*startled*)   I can't believe that.

Mrs Trevel   Yes, isn't that incredible. It does shock you, doesn't it. I can see.

But what interests me – what fascinates me, at this precise moment – is *you*. Is what happened between us. For some reason, I can't get that out of my mind.
Why do you think that is?

Slight pause.

Clare   Well, almost certainly because you've been through a very traumatic experience. Losing a child, not knowing where that child is – that is, obviously something very major . . .

Mrs Trevel *lights another cigarette.*

Mrs Trevel   Go on. (*She looks at* **Clare**.) Tell me more.

Very slight pause.

Clare   The first time I went to New York, at the age of eighteen, I was walking along by Central Park, I suddenly heard these yells, this terrible shouting. It was coming from a very tall man – and in front of him was this tiny girl, of about five. His daughter, he had evidently just that moment found her, after she'd wandered into the park alone.

And his whole body was shaking, and this huge man was literally screaming 'Never, never do that again', with such ferocity – I mean *really* terrifying. It was like he was completely possessed by rage and relief.
It's always been an indelible picture, a visual example for me of –

Mrs Trevel   Of the kind of thing I went through? And you think I've sort of got stuck in this rage and relief? It's an interesting idea . . . and I am taking it out on you?

Clare   No, that is not what I said.

Mrs Trevel   Like somehow I've got stuck, in third gear?

Pause. Pleasantly, softly.

You really think you're going to get away with just that?

Martin *enters with picnic. A large elegant hi-tech picnic basket.*

Clare   There you are . . . (*She turns.*) This is Martin Pender.

Mrs Trevel   The partner – we brushed past each other, didn't we, on that important day –

Martin   Hi. (*He is warmly polite.*) Nice to meet you.

He puts down the picnic basket, pointed smile at **Clare**.

I didn't realise you had company.

Turns back to **Mrs Trevel**, *who is looking closely at picnic basket. He watches this, pauses for a moment.*

Are you joining us? . . . Please join us.

Clare *has been trying to signal him not to do this.*

Mrs Trevel   Join the picnic? . . . You're too kind. (*She laughs.*) Maybe you should consult between yourselves. No, I won't barge in further.

Clare *relaxes for a second.*

Mrs Trevel   I'll just have one piece of fruit. If I may. A peach.

As **Martin** *hands her the fruit.*

I *love* that – a post-modernist picnic basket.

Martin   It's good, isn't it. (*He smiles.*) People covet it like mad.

Mrs Trevel   I'm sure. And a great spot for a picnic too . . . (*She gazes around.*) those white terraces . . .

Clare   Amazing aren't they – in the sun. I often wonder what goes on in them.

Mrs Trevel (*to* **Martin**)   So what do you do?

Martin   I'm an academic. Of a kind. A transport consultant.

Mrs Trevel   So to go with the sunbathing policemen and the head teachers . . . we have a transport consultant.

Martin (*puzzled by this*)   Quite. (*Then he smiles.*) I'm shortly to have a book published in fact. The result of several years labour – (*He laughs.*) too many years in fact!

Mrs Trevel   What is the book about?

Martin *hesitates.*

Martin   People usually miss a beat, when I tell them. The book is on – the Metrobus. The *London Metrobus*.

Mrs Trevel (*without missing a beat*)   Of course. Why not? (*She smiles.*) What is the London Metrobus?

Martin   It's the driver-only operated bus that has now taken over ninety-seven per cent of London routes. The sort you sit behind in your car, cursing, because you can't get by, waiting for all those people to lumber aboard and pay their fare.

Mrs Trevel Yes, I know that feeling, absolutely.

Martin Good. I was hoping you'd say that!

He is laying out the picnic, beginning to demonstrate his thesis with pieces of food.

To be strictly accurate there are two sorts of Metrobus, the Metrobus proper, and the LEYLAND TITAN, wonderful name isn't it, redolent of the seventies . . . I nearly used it as a title.

The thesis of the book is – it's the first major calculation ever of how many billions of pounds London has paid in congestion, in lost business hours, for taking a simple and idiotic decision to abolish the bus conductor!

Mrs Trevel Yes! Everybody in this city can follow that argument.

Martin Good. Yes! (*Encouraged by her interest.*) If this is a Metrobus (*With sandwich box.*) because of the extraordinary narrowness of the thoroughfares, the major arteries, in this town, and the fact that we don't have a set bus fare unlike almost every other Western capital, the whole of London is congealing. *The book shows the way forward.* (*He smiles.*) Now, the average Metrobus –

Clare Martin – Mrs Trevel can wait for the book to come out, I'm sure.

Martin Sorry. (*He grins.*) I can never resist a captive audience. (*Turns to* **Mrs Trevel**.) And what is your work?

Mrs Trevel 'My work'? (*She smiles.*) I don't do any at the moment – but I was once an Index Compiler. Or a Member of the Society of Indexers – to make it sound a little grander.

Martin Really? (*Lightly.*) You could have done my book then . . . !

Mrs Trevel Maybe. (*She blows smoke.*) If I was still practising . . . (*She looks at both of them.*)

When I've finished this peach, which I almost have – I will be gone.
It is idyllic, with the band playing.

Pause. She bends her head studying the ground.

Of course if you look on the ground . . . then you begin to see things, see what's happening in our parks, hypodermic needles, the inevitable used condoms, even some false teeth . . . it's gradually spreading . . . (*She smiles.*)

I even saw a rather muddy vibrator in the middle of the flower walk in Kensington Gardens, the other day.

She breaks off, moves slightly, glancing at the ground.

Sorry, I must stop peering around, I thought I saw something, (*She looks up.*) but it's obviously just –

Martin (*smiles*)   A form of displacement activity?

Mrs Trevel   I'm sure that's the right term. Yes.

Clare   Martin uses even more jargon than I do.

Slight pause.

Mrs Trevel   Delayed gratification . . .

Martin (*taken aback*)   Excuse me?

Mrs Trevel   Delayed gratification . . . that is one of my favourite pieces of jargon from your world, Miss Attwood, children having difficulty with . . . 'delayed gratification'.

Clare   When all we mean is they can't bloody wait for anything!

Mrs Trevel   That's right. Sometimes, occasionally, just for fun, I invent jargon. (*She smokes.*) 'Traumatic Overhang' . . . that kind of thing . . . 'Slow Lane Reversals' . . . children passing close to 'Dangerous' Information.

Clare   Well, 'Dangerous' Information is genuine jargon (*She smiles.*) I've even been known to use it. It's over emotive I agree.

Mrs Trevel   Yes. Well . . . (*She throws her finished peach stone into the litter bin.*) I've finished. Better begin to pick my way over all the basking flesh —
(*She smiles.*) I'll probably get arrested for having *too much* covered up!

She begins to move off.

Martin's *mobile phone begins to ring.* **Mrs Trevel** *stops and stares towards the ringing mobile in* **Martin**'s *pocket.*

Martin   It's all right, the bastards can wait. It's on the answer machine.

Pause.

Mrs Trevel   So, you've got one too.

Clare   Yes he has.

Mrs Trevel   For some reason, I don't know how I got the idea . . . just now I thought he was ringing from a call box, and you had *his* phone.

Clare (*calm, defiant*)   No.

Pause.

Mrs Trevel   It is an extraordinary time for professional people like you, isn't it?

I mean, in the old days, when you were out of the office, you were generally out of reach.
But there's the mobile culture now — and that vulnerable moment when you've just finished a call . . . and just about to make another, and it rings and *people can get through*.

She smokes.

So who gets the Mobile Number? Maybe nobody at all. But, perhaps you're the sort of person that *likes* to be available to certain *cases*, part of the service.

So then it becomes one measure — an important measure — of who gets put on the 'A' list.

Tough decisions have to be made. And then what lies, sometimes a whole spiral of little lies are necessary, aren't they, to keep particularly neurotic fuss-pots at bay. Like over protective middle-class mothers, who are demanding access which they patently don't deserve.

Clare   Mrs Trevel, what do you want? Tell me what I can do for you, now.

Mrs Trevel   These are clearly delicate problems – difficult to get right.

But if it goes wrong, you make a mistake – then it can only be temporarily embarrassing, awkward, but no more. One would have to be extremely unluckly, to get some sort of nutty avenging angel, coming at you all over town. Suddenly popping up everywhere, in the park, behind you on the escalators in the tube, or even in the bar, in the interval at the theatre.

Pause. Slight smile.

Yes, that would be unlucky, I agree.

She exits. Silence.

Martin   Jesus . . . !

Clare   Yes. Quite. (*She moves.*) FUCK, SHIT, FUCK, SHIT, FUCK FUCK! . . . Just thought I'd get that out!

Martin (*grins*)   I love it when you're analytical.

Clare   Well, I don't like being caught unawares! And what's more, *thanks* for inviting her to stay at the picnic.

Martin   What could I do? She was looking at the food! It was either that – or telling her to shove off. (*Smiles.*) Which might have been risky . . . !

Clare   Yes. But you were interested too, weren't you, in having a good peer at her.

Martin   I've heard a lot about this woman, it's natural to want to take a closer look.

Clare   Well, we certainly got one! (*Self-mocking smile.*) *And* she happens to appear when I'm stretched out half-naked! I could say this was all your fault . . .

Martin   No you couldn't!

Clare   No . . .

Pacing.

OK, you want a quick burst of analysis? Well, I DON'T
KNOW . . . I don't know what she's hoping to achieve. It
can't just be because she didn't get the attention she feels she
deserves. The phone calls and all that. Of course I feel guilty
about what happened – does she want that demonstrated
further? (*Sharp smile.*) Although it's far from clear what *did*
happen. She doesn't seem remotely concerned with the
reasons behind George's actions . . .

Maybe she exaggerated the whole disappearance – and he
was so embarrassed by his mother's behaviour – he wouldn't
come out of the woods! (*She moves.*) Maybe something is
going on in the marriage . . . if I could get to the husband
now – he seems a well-adjusted sort of character. Or even
better, if I could get *her* to see someone, a colleague.

Martin   No chance. There's no chance of that, *whatsoever*.

Clare   No. (*She moves.*) It'll burn itself out. A few more days
– and she'll begin to cool down.

Martin   You love it anyway. You love the challenge of it.
Whatever it is she's up to.

Clare (*mock rage*)   Don't you *dare* start on that – that's
rubbish.

Martin (*smiles*)   Right . . . OK . . . fine . . . (*Slight pause.*)
But you do . . .

Clare   No . . . (*She moves.*) And certainly not in this case.

Martin *watches her, smiles.*

Clare   Well, come on – we've only got a few minutes more
of this picnic, it's all she's left us.

She smiles. Starts eating.

I couldn't help thinking of George, and the way he's always
finding money on the pavement. And there SHE is,

surveying the ground in all these parks, and finding RUDE LITTER! It must be in the genes.

She touches **Martin**, *warm, teasing.*

Come on then – are you going to give me some calm, dispassionate advice?

Martin   Advice! . . . *You* want advice?

Clare   Why not?

Martin (*grins*)   Right . . . (*Slight pause.*) Run like hell in the opposite direction!

Clare (*warm laugh*)   OK . . . Great.

Martin   So are you going to advise me about the Book Launch?

Clare   Book '*launch*' . . . I didn't realise it was going to be that showbizzy!

Martin   A volume on the Metrobus – what do you think? (*He laughs.*) One can but dream! No – I don't mind if nobody reads it. I don't. (*Slight pause.*) It's really solid, like its subject. (*Serious.*) It's the *work, that counts.* (*Forceful.*) *It is.*

Clare *warm, touching him.*

Clare   Absolutely! That's right.

Blackout.

Scene Three – A

Clare *standing in long coat.*

Clare   Jess – on FAME.

(*As Jess.*) It's not worth it. Take it from me – it's just not worth it.

I came round the corner the other day in Soho – it was just off Wardour Street.
There were a whole lot of photographers, crowded together

like flies – round this model or actress. And suddenly she spins round and she's holding up her hands, like this!

She does it palms outwards.

And they're covered in blood! Yeah – fake blood – I'm sure – but blood! And she starts screaming at them . . . freaking them, their mouths wide open, and she's holding up her bloody hands right in their faces! (*She does it again.*)

I don't know who she was – but she's gone completely crackers, already!

She sits.

And GEORGE, on FAME.

(*As George.*) My English master, Mr Brownjohn, gets really cross about this radio programme *Desert Island Discs* – do you know it? Where famous people get asked to choose music they'd like to play at sea.

He comes in on Monday mornings and says I can't BELIEVE who was on *Desert Island Discs* yesterday. They haven't done nearly enough to deserve to be on! He says. It's an absolute disgrace, why on earth did they invite that person, he's NOTHING! My teacher gets so *angry* – he says he's going to write and complain because it makes a nonsense of the whole thing.

Pause.

Do you think Mr Brownjohn will ever get on it?

Scene Four

Clare's office. **Gina** *brushing her hair, ready to go out.* **Richard** *sitting watching her.*

Gina   She won't be long.

Richard   Good. (*Slight pause.*) I can wait. I'm very used to waiting here.

He looks across at **Gina**, *as she puts her make-up on. Her very contained manner.*

You're very different to Mrs Haggerty.

Gina   I'm sure I am.

Richard   She was here in my time, she seemed very old then. I expect she was only fifty.
All the kids would sulk while they waited, I know *I* did, and the parents looking a bit ashamed . . . thinking 'OH my God I hope nobody walks in who knows me!' The English are by far the worst about this, aren't they – about having their children 'seen to' –

Gina (*brisk*)   That's not true any more – it's getting much better.

Richard   Right! . . . (*Glancing around.*) And Mrs Haggerty sat over there, and she just chatted all the time, really cheery, never stopped.

Gina   I don't tend to chatter.

Richard   No. (*He grins.*) I think I'd worked that out.

He gets up, moves over to her.

Where are you going tonight?

Slight pause.

Gina   Out with friends.

Richard   Out with friends . . . Ah! (*He smiles.*) That sounds promising.

Close to her. Flirting with her.

Maybe you completely change – after a certain hour. Suddenly this exotic, incredibly daring person appears . . . this creature of the night! (*Teasing smile.*) Is that what happens?

Gina   That's not quite how I'd describe it. (*Slight pause.*) But I know how to enjoy myself.

Richard   That's great . . . I know how to do that too! I think I'm pretty good at it by now. (*Watching her contained manner.*) So how *do* you enjoy yourself? . . . Lots of drugs? . . . Frenzied karaoke? . . . Or maybe sitting at the computer sending masses of seductive e-mail all over the world?

Pause.

Gina   I have been known to do two of those three.

Richard (*very curious*)   Really . . . ?

Gina   Yes. (*She looks straight at him.*) And *one* of them rather often.

She moves across the room.

Richard   I went to a Rave for the first time, the other night. They're already out of date apparently, maybe this was the last one! . . . It was behind the gasworks in King's Cross. People were dancing in weird ways.

He imitates.

Looked very strange to me . . . and sometimes they did a little flourish, with their hands – that reminded me of my parents dancing, when I was tiny. It was very unsexy – but what do I know? . . . I've only been in America. (*He grins.*) Nothing happens there!

Clare *enters in smart evening-dress, she is wearing earrings.*

Clare   There you are, Richard.

Richard   You haven't forgotten?

Clare   Of course not.

Richard   You look amazing. What's it for? Where are you going?

Clare   Oh, it's just a fund-raising function, rather formal, it's for a children's charity.

Richard   Everybody's heading somewhere? Why not? It's a great summer's evening out there.

Clare (*turning*)   So, Gina – you can go now. Have a good time.

Gina   Thanks. I think I will. If it all goes according to plan.

Gina exits.

Richard (*laughs*)   'Goes to plan' – she's a funny girl, isn't she!

Clare   She's very good at her job. She's just extremely self-contained.

Richard   You look really great in that dress!

Clare   Thank you.

Richard   You should have looked like that during our sessions!

Slight pause. **Clare** *smiles.*

Clare   So, Richard . . .

Richard   Where to begin?

Clare   I don't know. (*Lightly.*) Where are you going to begin?

Richard   I want to fill you in about America – it was great! I did well, I think, on the course.

Clare   Naturally. You were always a very bright boy.

Richard   I brought some pictures. Where are they? (*Shuffling in his pockets.*) I know other people's pictures are the most boring things in the world. So for you, it's selected highlights! A few of my friends, several cross-country journeys, a couple of landmark moments. (*He smiles.*) It was an interesting time . . . I want to do it justice.

About to show photos, **Gina** *enters.*

Clare   Yes, Gina.

Gina   I've got bad news. Well, it may be bad news – Mrs Trevel is here.

Clare *NO*. She can't do this now. Not again. I have an appointment. Tell her, I have an appointment.

Gina I was literally just going out, and as the door opened – she was there.

Clare *I will not see her*.

Gina I couldn't stop her – she pushed past. She must have been waiting for the moment.

Mrs Trevel *enters carrying a very large box-briefcase, and two other bags.*

Mrs Trevel Yes – I pushed past. But it's OK I can wait, I'll wait outside. (*Indicating* **Richard**.) You can deal with him first, if you like.

Clare I cannot see you now, Mrs Trevel, it is out of the question. We can discuss making an appointment, for some time later – but I am simply not able –

Mrs Trevel (*calmly*) Oh yes you are.

Richard Yes, yes. You do *her*.

Clare Richard, *you're* the one with an appointment.

Richard *is taking in* **Mrs Trevel**'s *appearance with all her bags.*

Richard No, no please. I'd rather not have somebody waiting to come in. Pacing around outside. The conditions have to be right to do this. I'll go for a walk. No, I will, and come back and see how you're doing.

Clare Ten minutes, Richard!

Richard Oh yeah . . . less. (*As he exits.*) You have a good time now.

Mrs Trevel What a handsome boy! One of your old clients? Come back to see you? Must be good when that happens, pleasing, when they *want* to see you.

Clare *watching* **Mrs Trevel** *closely.*

Clare Yes it is.

Gina Would you like me to stay, Miss Attwood?

Very slight pause.

Clare   No, Gina, that's not necessary. You go off for your evening.

Gina *looks across at* **Mrs Trevel**.

Gina   Actually I've just remembered I've got a phone call to make, so I'll be out there for a short while.

Gina *hesitates and then leaves.*

Mrs Trevel (*smiles*)   She's going to wait . . . she's worried about you. (*Moves.*) Of course, you can always get her to drag me out of here.

Clare (*unfazed*)   Let's hope she doesn't have to do that.

Mrs Trevel *moves purposefully into the middle of the stage, sits and opens the large briefcase with a very loud click. It is stuffed with papers and files, which she begins to spread in stacks, around her chair.*

Mrs Trevel (*as she does this*)   You look splendid, dressed like that. A successful busy woman, and you still manage to look elegant, unhurried.

Clare   I'm going out later, to a function. My partner is picking me up.

Mrs Trevel   Your partner . . . (*She smiles.*) He's always turning up on time, isn't he? You obviously have a deeply convenient relationship.

Clare *watching her.*

Clare (*sharp*)   We happen to have an engagement tonight, that is why this is not a good time –

Mrs Trevel *suddenly looks up.*

Mrs Trevel   Look, I think we crossed over a boundary, didn't we, in the park. At least *I* feel we did. And now it's time – to use that awful expression – for the gloves to come off.

Clare   So you feel you're in a fight, do you, Mrs Trevel?

The briefcase and files being organised, crisp noises.

Mrs Trevel   Just need to get this ready . . . I know you're wondering how big a pickle you're in.

Clare (*calmly*)   Am I in a pickle?

Mrs Trevel   Any moment –

Clare   Mrs Trevel, if you want to complain about me, if you think I've done my job badly, there's a structure to deal with that, there is an ethics committee –

Mrs Trevel *looks up innocently.*

Mrs Trevel   This isn't about whether you're good at your job, Miss Attwood. Whether you were giving the right treatment . . . It's more interesting . . .
I think you're probably a fair to good practitioner, middle of the road, not too stupidly dogmatic about following just *one* approach, either being a Kleinian or whatever the other one was called . . . isn't that so?

Clare   I *try* not to be over doctrinaire.

Mrs Trevel   Good. (*She is poised, ready.*) So, you asked me in the park, *what I* wanted.
And I have thought of one thing I want from you. For all the children you deal with – you compile files, don't you? I'm sure they're considered highly secret. I want the files that you keep on George.

Slight pause.

Clare   You know I can't give you those Mrs Trevel.

Mrs Trevel *looks across at her.*

Mrs Trevel (*calmly*)   I think you will give them to me, by the time I finish.

The papers spread around her.

I've got something here which I want to use, to show you.

Because I realise I must seem like the Mother from Hell to you – I hate that expression too – but it probably accurately sums up what you think of me. And I thought you were entitled, to a couple of illustrations of why I was behaving like I am . . . OK.

Clare *watching her*.

Clare And what have you got there?

Mrs Trevel This is what *I* consider – 'dangerous information'.

Clare Dangerous information! About what? About me?

Mrs Trevel No no. (*She laughs.*) Is there some? No, no, it's not about you, Miss Attwood . . . !
'Dangerous information' means, doesn't it, information that could be difficult or confusing for that child to cope with?

She moves papers around.

This is dangerous information that George sees.

She holds up newspapers.

Firstly, this is a well-known *broadsheet* newspaper. On the day, the very day, a child serial killer is found guilty and it is all over the front page, a truly *terrible* story. On the back page of the *same* newspaper there's the cheerful headline, a trailer for a feature, 'HAD ENOUGH OF SERIAL KILLER CHIC . . . ?'

She looks up from the paper.

Isn't that extraordinary?

Clare Yes . . . I can't really respond, Mrs Trevel, until I know where you're heading.

Mrs Trevel (*watching her*) Doesn't it show you how everything is sliding together, news and entertainment, one great big wash of ephemeral rubbish.
My husband, who is an accountant, not a literary man, but he likes to coin expressions – he's not particularly good at it, but he does it. (*Waves newspaper.*) And he calls this phenomenon '*Gleaze*' . . . sleaze and glitter. Everywhere, things are merging.

Some papers flutters off her across stage.

Oh dear, there goes another piece of dangerous information.
Let's leave it there for a moment, ticking away.
Come to this one – Market Testing.

She holds up a form.

This is a market-testing questionnaire from when George
and I visited our local toy museum. It is asking the question
'Is the museum correctly oriented' – strange phrasing I agree
– 'towards the right market – Is it properly targeted?'
As we walked away together, George said,
'Mummy, am *I* correctly oriented towards the right market?'

Clare   I don't believe he said that, I think that story's
fiction.

Mrs Trevel   *He definitely said it.* It made me realise we'll
soon be market researching our children immediately
they're in the womb, identifying the niche for them to aim
for, and seeing which genes need a bolstering.

Clare   Mrs Trevel, I have parents all the time obsessed
about giving their children the right start. Talking about
moving house immediately to live next door to the best
school, or even creating false addresses to make sure their
child gets in. I have them agonising about the *food* they're
giving their children, a *whole* fake industry is growing up of
potions and special foods to make your child into a new
improved human being –

Mrs Trevel (*slight smile*)   You're responding now? You
think you know where I'm heading?

Clare   – And I tell all these parents, in a variety of ways but
I tell them, there is time. There IS time. Slow down. And
they do.

Watching **Mrs Trevel** *with papers.*

And so should you.

Silence. **Mrs Trevel** *is immersed in the big briefcase, seemingly
oblivious. Papers fluttering everywhere.*

Mrs Trevel   I'm looking for something very small. (*A paper shoots across stage.*) Whoops, there goes another! We'll leave that there for a moment.

She rummages.

Small and *yellow* . . .
I think it's in this bag. (*Plunging into her handbag.*) There are little leftovers here from our holiday in America, (*Lightly.*) a few dollars, this mace . . . (*Produces can.*) you know the spray for blinding muggers . . . Is it illegal, by the way, to carry that in this country?

Momentary pause.

Clare   Yes. It is. I should get rid of it if I was you.

Mrs Trevel   Yes, well, I wouldn't need this on a summer night in London, surely! (*Pleasant laugh.*) Don't look like that . . . your assistant is standing guard outside after all! (*Blithely.*) Then again, maybe a little frisson between us is good.

Very slight pause, she puts the mace down in front of her on the table. She then produces a tiny yellow newspaper cutting.

So here it is.

Clare   *That's* what you were looking for?

Mrs Trevel   (*holding it tight*)   So this is the Future – I cut it out and kept it as soon as I read it.

She is about to read it then stops.

You know what worries me most, how confident everybody is when they pontificate about the New Technology. About how paradise is just round the corner, especially for children – able to 'communicate'.

Clare   It *is* second nature for most kids now, the new technology.

Mrs Trevel   Really? That's what they all say. Even the actual words, Internet, Superwhatnot, Cyberspace, sound frightfully smug, don't they, pleased with themselves?

She smoothes out the yellow cutting.

The only thing we can be *certain* about is – people are ALWAYS wrong about the future.

Clare   But *you* were just telling me how people would treat their pregnancies in the future.

Mrs Trevel (*smiles*)   Naturally I am the exception. (*She indicates cutting.*) This is how the future seemed in 1971 and they were so sure . . .

'By nineteen ninety-eight, MASS AIR TRAVEL WILL BE A THING OF THE PAST' . . . !

She looks up incredulous.

– 'the cost of criss-crossing the globe will have become prohibitively expensive because of energy costs . . . This will lead to the REBIRTH of indigenous cultures – and a consequent decrease in violence.' Amazing, isn't it!

Clare   You must be one of the very few people that keeps predictions –

Mrs Trevel (*continuing to quote*)   'Young children will be able to walk the streets with ease, without any fear for their safety.'

She throws cutting back into her bag.

In other words, a return to the safe world of my childhood . . . when it was so much, undoubtedly so very much –

Clare   No. *No.*

Mrs Trevel   What do you mean, no?

Clare   I mean, no, that is wrong. This is the Golden Age of Childhood argument, the recent past was so much better. I'm afraid if there's one thing I'm sick of hearing it's that myth being peddled. I really am. Every other parent I see comes out with it.

Mrs Trevel   But it *was* so much easier and *safer* when I was a child –

Clare   Since I know you don't like jargon, Mrs Trevel –
that is bullshit, utter crap.

Mrs Trevel (*startled quiet*)   I can't believe you think that.

Clare *moving over to drawer*.

Clare   I want you to hear something. Children had very
real fear then. Worse maybe . . . listen to this.
I want you to listen to this child.

Mrs Trevel   So you *tape* all the children as well . . . whose
child is this?

Clare *produces old tape-recorder from drawer with tape already on it.*

Clare (*switching it on*)   An old tape-recorder . . . for an old
tape.

A soft young **Girl's voice** *starts, with a slight Lancashire accent.*
The **Girl's voice** *is half a whisper, very private in tone. There is the*
sound of music, a pop song from the early sixties, behind her voice and
the sound of a family around on the stairs. The effect is intensely
evocative, laughter from somebody outside the door, voices of a family
half heard.

Girl's voice (*secretive*)   In one moment I'll do it, Dad is just
on the stairs – just got to wait for him to go down. So there's
no chance of anybody coming in . . .

Mrs Trevel   What a lovely voice . . . who is this child?

Slight pause.

Clare   The only child I can play without asking anyone –
it's me . . . at the age of ten and a half.

Mrs Trevel   It doesn't sound like you at all.

Clare   My family had just come down from the North,
from Stockport. The year before. You can hear my accent
just beginning to go . . .

A man's voice butts in to the room for a moment, the girl answers.

Mrs Trevel   And that's your father?

Clare   Yes. (*She listens to her father calling.*) There he is . . .

Mrs Trevel   A nice warm voice.

Clare *stops the tape for a moment.*

Clare   I kept an audio diary, I used to play music with it, snatches of my favourite records, and then things from the radio, compile little items of my own. (*Slight laugh.*) The days before the video diary . . . I tried to make sense of the world on tape.

She plays tape.

Now listen, please.

Girl's voice   I'm afraid . . . I can't get it out of my head. I'm very afraid they're going to let off the BOMB, really soon. Blow up everything, scorch my school, the end of all the buildings I know, melt the playground. *SSShhh* . . . hang on a moment.

Sixties music from tape.

Mrs Trevel   This is very strange, it really is . . . listening to this with you. Eavesdropping – on you as a girl.

Girl's voice (*continues*)   We drove past a golf course yesterday, Mum and Dad, and Sarah and me. These men strutting about – I imagined them all being fried, as they played golf, caught by the flash, burnt to a cinder like toast. But still standing up, standing absolutely still like sentries, all these burnt golfers – and the whole course completely, really really black. As far as I could see . . . (*Her voice hushed.*) It was *frightening*.

Clare *stops the tape.*

Mrs Trevel   No, don't do that, please – don't stop it. (*The tape restarts.*) The music, it's so good . . . hearing that music. It's probably playing on the same sort of cheap red gramophone I had.

Clare   I usually stop here. It's just some singing now . . . me humming to my records.

Mrs Trevel   No, please leave it just for a second – . . . doesn't it really get to you? It gives me goose-pimples . . .

being transported back into the past like that. (*As the singing continues*.) We must be roughly the same age, (*She smiles*.) though tonight you look much younger than me of course. But it is the *same* music, I listened to.

Clare I'm just aware of my rather off-key 'singing', if you can call it that. The previous part of the tape is what's interesting –

Mrs Trevel I know I know. But listen . . .

She is moving, very intrigued, the music stops for a second.

Other sounds from outside the girl's room, fill the tape and the auditorium.
She suddenly turns.

My God – did you hear that? And again . . . ! *That?*

Clare What?

Mrs Trevel That hiss . . . there. That sort of spitting hiss . . . ! Don't you hear it?

Clare (*startled*) A hiss?

Mrs Trevel It's a TROLLEYBUS! It is, that sound there. I promise you! An extinct trolleybus – it's passing right under your window.

The noise brushing close.

Oh my God, that does make me almost shake . . . I haven't heard that sound, not since, since I was a girl.

For a moment the sound moves all around us, and then begins to recede.

Clare Yes, well, it was probably the last trolleybus running through Acton . . . its final journey!

Mrs Trevel You can almost smell the leather, can't you? See the young girls chattering together, and those big tickets you got given, for the old dark pennies. And all those fat stubby cars of your youth . . .

The music comes back.

You stopped to change a record, as a girl, and *there* was that sound, in the gap, coming out of that street at us. And so *clear* . . .

Hear the ringing too . . . ? Very faint, there! That belongs to one of those sleepy old police cars – charging somewhere.

Pause. The sounds slip away.

That was great . . . !

As the music resumes playing.

I feel an overpowering urge sometimes – I just want to go back to that time so much! I'm terrible about the past . . . (*As the girl sings.*) Want to climb back into it . . . When everything was easy, the future was bright, there was a job round every corner if you wanted it . . .

She turns.

Wouldn't you want to go back to that time? Even briefly?

Clare   No. Absolutely not.

She walks towards the tape, as her young self sings out. The singing getting louder.

I was in a tiny room, right next to the loo. I had a lot of nightmares in that little bed. And outside that window – the world seemed rather dangerous.
As I think I've tried to show you.

She stops the tape.

And now you really must allow me to continue with what I was doing. Richard is coming back at any moment.

Mrs Trevel   Yes, where is he? –

Clare   And Martin is picking me up soon –

Mrs Trevel   But for the moment we're alone. I expect your assistant's left by now. (*Calmly.*) Now, are you going to give me the files I want? On George.

Clare   No, of course not. I thought I made that clear. But there's really nothing that important in those files, you should put them out of your mind. (*Slight pause.*)

Mrs Trevel (*calmly*)   I know you think I'm a rather old-fashioned sort of person, you do, don't you, an under-employed mother who has nothing better to fill her days than constantly fussing about her children. But you're wrong. That is not the case.

Please give me the files.

Clare   No. It would set a precedent that could have all sorts of implications.

Facing her.

Mrs Trevel, you can try the law if you like. You can try litigation – no doubt we're going the American way and there will be litigation about absolutely everything. Just as over there, nobody apparently is responsible for any of their actions – if you murder your parents it must be because they abused you, even if you can't remember them doing it. Or because your favourite game show was suddenly rescheduled!
And if your child runs away, it must be because the therapist wasn't at the end of the phone! But finally we have to look *inside*, not at all these external matters, but look at ourselves.

Mrs Trevel   So you're not going to give me anything? . . . I see.

Clare   So – now if you could . . .

Mrs Trevel   You think you've handled this pretty well, don't you? Risen to the challenge?

Suddenly she swings round.

You LIED to me. (*Coming at* **Clare**.) *And what's worse, you just lied to me again!*

Clare (*very startled*)   What? I *haven't* just lied to you –

Mrs Trevel   Yes you have. What *is* the point. WHAT IS THE POINT IF YOU DO THIS! TELL ME? YOU KEEP LYING TO ME.

Suddenly she hits **Clare**, *glancing blows.* **Clare** *turning away as she comes for her.* **Clare** *manages to catch hold of her arms, powerfully restraining her.*

Clare   Mrs Trevel, just calm down (*Really strong.*) YOU'RE GOING TO CALM DOWN NOW.

Mrs Trevel's *eruption subsides. She breaks away.*

Mrs Trevel   Yes, yes . . . (*Slight smile.*) very sound advice. (*Pause, she laughs.*) I must be stuck in that third gear, mustn't I. (*She moves.*) She's absolutely BARKING, that's what you're thinking . . . (*Slight pause.*) I'm sorry.

Pause. She faces her.

You're such a clever woman, Miss Attwood, I mean a genuinely impressive person. Maybe a little arrogant, but imaginative, and not really that aloof, unlike a lot of people in your position.

Why is it, that I feel so strongly I've got to finish you – finish your career? To put it at its crudest – to do my best to reduce you to nothing.

Pause.

Clare (*startled, quiet*)   I had no idea that is what you were trying to do, Mrs Trevel. (*Slight pause.*) But it will seem different in a few days, it will be less intense.

Mrs Trevel   You think things will change in the morning? Maybe you're right . . . (*She moves. Pause. She smiles.*) I admit what I'm trying to do is pretty difficult.

Martin *enters. He is wearing a fashionable suit.*

Mrs Trevel   He arrives. Not on a white horse, but he arrives. As you said he would.

Martin (*surprised*)   Hello . . . Mrs Trevel.

Mrs Trevel *straightening her hair, her head bent.*

Martin   Are you all right?

Mrs Trevel   Yes . . . (*She moves, pause, smokes.*) What a display . . . ! (*Pause.*) It'll sound a bit ridiculous if I say, have a good evening . . . but have a good evening.

She exits. Silence.

Clare (*quiet*)   That is one rather disturbed lady . . .

Martin   You mean she's fucking crazy, that's what you mean!

Clare   If you like . . . she just went for me, just before you arrived, semi-attacked me.

Martin   Really? Are you OK? (*Coming up to her.*) What did she do?

Clare   I'm fine . . . (*She smiles.*) . . . I think! No, it's all right . . . When she tries to bludgeon her way to what she wants it's easy to deal with.
(*Pacing.*) I'm definitely going to involve some colleagues. Make sure George is all right, bombard her with letters, *try* to get her to see someone.

Martin   Yes!

Pause.

Clare   It's as if I've become every professional to her – every lawyer she's had to deal with, every teacher, every doctor . . . It's like she wants to bag one, take out a professional. (*Warm smile at* **Martin**.) Talking of which – you look good.

Martin   Yes. (*Grins.*) I like it too. I thought I'd wear this for the great presentation. Don't look so blank! You know at the Queen Elizabeth Conference Centre – World-wide transport conference. *My lecture.* I'm beginning to think it's time for me to develop a rather more svelte look.

Clare (*warm smile*)   You should . . . (*She moves.*) Richard never came back. You didn't see him? I wonder what happened . . .

She is moving towards tape machine. Quiet.

She can't get me, can she?

Martin   Get you? You mean do you harm professionally?
Mrs Trevel! Of course not.

Clare   No, I don't see how she could . . . there's no legal
way . . .

Thinking about it softly.

I don't see what she can do . . . (*She smiles.*) Anyway, I'm up
to it. (*Self mocking laugh.*) After all she even promoted me,
during the session, from a 'fair to good practitioner' to a
'genuinely impressive person'!

She switches on tape, her younger self softly humming to pop tune.

Martin (*studying an A–Z closely*)   It's such a great night out
there, I thought we could walk to this 'do'. I've been working
out a way to get to Lincoln's Inn Fields, taking in a couple of
interesting places on the way, a couple of really obscure
crannies, one of which I've never even heard of . . . ! It has
the most wonderful name, Long Lost Yard . . . I've planned
an elaborate –

He looks up.

Who's this? What's this tape?

Clare *standing by tape.*

Clare   Oh, it's just from a few years back.

Pause.

It's only a girl singing.

Her young self continues to hum along to the record.

Fade.

Act Two

Scene One

Hot strong sunlight.

Clare *is standing by her desk, three Plasticine figures like misshapen dolls standing in a row on the desk. Two of them are dressed in clothes, bits of old denim etc., one of them is still wrapped up in dirty newspaper, completely covered.* **Clare** *faces us.*

Clare   I came in a few days ago – and these squat little figures were waiting for me . . . wrapped up in newspaper, standing in a line on my desk.
They are in fact rather sturdily made, out of grubby Play-doh.
Later that day Jess turned up, for an appointment. Bang on time as always.

She begins to unwrap third Plasticine figure.

(*As Jess.*) I see you've only unwrapped two of them – what are you trying to tell me? . . . they're no good?

By the way, what did you think of Marble Arch? – Best one yet, wasn't it?
Did I tell you, when I dropped it off, I met your partner, I really hate using that fucking word – I expect *you* do too . . .
But you probably *have* to use it, don't you! Anyway, I met your 'partner', your boyfriend, your bloke – he's just right for you, isn't he – a bit shaggy, really calm and soothing, but quite funny . . . in a laid-back way. And he was really interested in my models. Yes!

Third figure coming out of newspaper.

And when I've told you about *these* – you'll want them on your mantelpiece, at home. You will!

Moving, holding the figure.

You see, I thought, let's look at this place – like the tourists do. See the city as they see it.

So first – we've got to call the policemen 'Bobbies' (*Pronouncing it with ludicrous American/Cockney accent.*) – the only people to use the word BOBBIES are Americans – like they say 'Where are your cute London BOBBIES . . . ?' (*She smiles.*) And you don't know what the fuck they're talking about . . .

And the second thing – YOU HAVE TO GO TO MADAME TUSSAUDS. Oh Yes . . . ! You know, the wax museum.

Because every time you pass there, it doesn't matter what day of the year it is – there's a truly FUCKING ENORMOUS QUEUE. Have you noticed that? – There is ALWAYS a queue. *All tourists.*

And for that reason – nobody that actually *lives* in London has been inside that wax museum for years and years and years . . . ! Anything could be going on in there, couldn't it!?

So – *I* went inside. I did. Just sneaked round the front of the queue, it was dead easy.

And you know what I saw . . . ? It was a very hot day . . . And all these models, the wax models, they were beginning to MELT.

The Prime Minister had shrunk a bit, one ear had run down the side of his chin . . . Prince Charles's face was sort of sinking into his chest, so the top was just one big misshapen ball, and the American President – he was going at the waist, and one of his legs was melting smaller, and curling round, so it was like a little tail.

No point you looking like that – you haven't been in the BLOODY PLACE have you? . . . since you were ten probably! So you have no idea what's happening there . . . so shut up!

And I thought – stuff all these Politicians and 'Pop Performers' . . . ! They should have a room, about my age group, about the FUTURE.
Yeah. You know the 'Football fan of the future' with his

machine gun held next to his football scarf, that sort of thing, and the 'Schoolkid of the future', with her porno virtual reality goggles for when she's playing in the playground.

So there we are − (*She lines up the three figures.*) that's who they are. The funny thing is − you're ever so cool when I show you these things, you think that'll stop me bringing them to you . . . make us talk deeply instead − about my *insides*. But it just makes me bring them all the more.

Clare *exits. The light changes, soft sunlight.*

Martin, **Gina**, *bustling around.* **Martin** *quite animated and nervous.*

Clare *enters − breezy, relaxed, moving over to her desk.*

Martin   So, Clare − here's your ticket. Put it somewhere really obvious, safe, *now*. Are you clear which entrance you should go to?

Clare   Absolutely, (*She smiles.*) don't worry.

Gina   It's your big day, Mr Pender.

Martin (*grins, trying to hide his nerves*)   My 'big day', Gina, yes. (*He looks at her.*) Pity you can't be there too . . .

Gina (*flatly*)   That is a pity, Mr Pender. Yeah.

Martin (*laughs*)   You'll be able to watch the highlights, when they bring out the video.

He moves.

The most important lecture of my life − and it is scheduled for the Friday afternoon before the August bank holiday!

Clare   Everybody will stay for it. Don't worry. (*Warm smile.*) How could they not . . .

Martin   All *two thousand* delegates? Maybe! Even the representatives from Macedonia . . . ? (*He laughs.*) All going to get the full benefit of my encyclopaedic knowledge of the London Metrobus . . . !

Gina   Will they be interested? In the Metrobus? − I mean the people from Macedonia?

Clare (*smiles*)   Of course they will. Anyway, it's a great launching pad for your book.

Martin   Yes. And at least nobody will be able to shout back – I absolutely disagree! What a load of bollocks, you've got it all wrong! For this afternoon at least I will be the acknowledged world expert, on the Leyland Titan! (*He smiles.*) And how we went wrong organising the city's transport.

He turns to **Clare**.

Did I mention you need to be there about twenty minutes before I'm on? Better make that half an hour. And I'm on at *15.15* – which is –

Clare   I know. I know! Yes. I'll be there. (*Warm smile.*) Don't *worry*.

Martin (*producing booklet*)   Yes . . . I'm on just after the Canadians and their talk – 'Mono-rails, Dead or Alive?' (*He moves.*) I'm going off to rehearse now, in a quiet back passage at the conference centre. I've just been going over 'The Insiders guide to the REALLY BIG Public Address'. (*Laughs.*) It's made me even more nervous! Don't use all your best jokes right at the beginning, it's that kind of thing. And introduce a *pause* exactly ONE THIRD of the way in, a sort of stumbling incompetent pause, like you've completely forgotten what happens next – makes them all sit up in an instant apparently. (*Smiles.*) Electrifies the bastards.

Clare (*going up to him*)   It'll be OK, it really will.

Gina   Best of luck, Mr Pender.

Martin   Yes. (*He kisses* **Clare**.) Well, you'll probably find you're sitting directly in my eyeline . . . maybe that'll be a good thing! I'll do it all for you . . . it'll give it a personal feel.

Clare   Right. (*Warm laugh.*) And I'll be mouthing back, it's going great.

Martin (*grins*)   I'm going to give them something to remember! (*He exits.*)

Clare   Right. (*She moves back to her papers, to herself.*) Put my ticket exactly where I can find it. Good.

Gina   Shall I move these . . . ? (*She hesitates by the 'dolls', disapprovingly.*) These figures – ?

Clare   Yes. If you could. (*Sharp.*) Not *those* ones!

Gina *is moving two brown boxes that are also on the desk.*

Clare   Those are some personal things from my father's. From his old office.

Gina (*putting them back*)   Sorry. I didn't realise.

Clare   Yes – I don't know why it's taken eight months after his death, for them to let me have them. But there we are. I picked them up this morning from the solicitor – *he kept me waiting*, naturally. I parked in the underground car park, in Marble Arch. Can you remember that? –

Gina   Yes, Miss Attwood.

Clare   Because I was running late – I left the car there. It will have been there all day. You will remind me, Gina, that's where it is?

Gina   Yes. I will.

Clare   Great. (*Her mood breezy, relaxed.*) So, I've just got a short talk with Mr Boulton – what does he want I wonder? – and then Richard's rearranged appointment, and then you're *free*, Gina.

Gina   Yes.

Clare   Another chance to get out of town. What are you doing *this* holiday weekend? Going somewhere, got something special laid on?

Gina   Oh, this and that. Watering the window box . . . getting in some Chinese food – (*Slight pause.*) and maybe something else.

Clare (*warm laugh*)   That sounds nice and mysterious! Tell me. Just for a change, tell me, Gina.

Slight pause. **Gina** *hesitates.*

(*Warm smile.*) Or tell me half? How about that? (*Trying to be friendly.*) Is that a deal?

Very slight pause.

Gina   I'd rather not. If you don't mind. (*She moves.*) If it's all the same to you. (*Slight pause.*) Excuse me, I thought I heard the bell . . .

Gina *exits.* **Clare** *smiles. She opens one of her father's boxes, peers in, takes out a dusty old sixties office toy. Silver balls that knock together. She gives them an amused look.*

Gina *enters.*

Gina   Mr Boulton is here.

Boulton *enters, carrying a large bag. A beat behind him,* **Mrs Trevel** *enters. She is dressed in summer clothes, she seems far more relaxed, dark glasses, her hair different, much more attractively dressed.* **Gina** *watches for second, then exits.*

Clare (*to* **Boulton**)   Hello . . . (*Then she sees* **Mrs Trevel**.) Mrs Trevel! What are you doing here? This is *Mr Boulton's* appointment.

Mrs Trevel   I know. (*Breezily.*) That's all right.

Boulton   If you don't mind – I would very much like Mrs Trevel to be here.

Clare *looks from one to another.*

Clare   For what purpose?

Mrs Trevel (*sitting demurely in corner*)   I'd be very interested if I could sit in, if I may . . . ?

Boulton   Yes –

Clare   I'm afraid all appointments with me are completely confidential –

Boulton   But this is not a private matter. It doesn't concern *Leo.* This is more social . . . it'd just help me if Mrs Trevel was here.

Mrs Trevel (*low laugh*)   Bet that surprises you!

Boulton   *Please.*

Slight pause.

Clare   Well, only if it has nothing to do with Leo, and if that's the case I'm not really sure why we're meeting . . .

Boulton   Thank you. She can stay? That's very good of you.

Clare   But if there's *anything* that does touch on Leo (*To* **Mrs Trevel**.) – I will have to ask you to leave, immediately.

Boulton   Of course. We understand.

Clare   And I haven't a lot of time. My partner is giving a lecture later today, which I have to attend, and I have various things to do before then . . .

Pause. **Boulton** *looks at her.*

Boulton   So . . . Now . . .

He hesitates.

What I want to do will surprise you, I think. May seem a trifle odd, initially (*He smiles.*) you may even think I've taken leave of my senses.

Clare (*trying to keep the atmosphere relaxed, laughs*)   This is some build up, Mr Boulton – what could you possibly have in mind?

Boulton   Yes, well – (*He laughs.*) it's not what typically happens in here! It'll seem like excessive behaviour . . . (*Smiles.*) But in fact it's not. All I ask, you bear with me, for just a few moments, because it will *become* crystal clear, in a minute, what I'm trying to demonstrate.

Clare   Of course . . .

Boulton   And this is one of the reasons for Mrs Trevel being here, to help me with the tasting.

Clare (*startled*)   The tasting?

Mrs Trevel (*laughs*)   The tasting . . . sounds promising, doesn't it!

Boulton *reaches into his bag and takes out a package. Inside, done up with string, is a fistful of Cadbury Flakes.*

Clare (*smiling*)   Chocolate . . .

Boulton   Yes, the Chocolate Flake – one of the great pieces of confectionery, I think we'll agree, ever created. An icon even, in the world of cheap chocolate. And its date? When do you think it dates from . . . ? Yes, go on, guess! (*Unable to wait.*) I'll tell you, 1920!

Clare   Really? I had no idea. That's much earlier than I would have guessed.

Boulton   Yes, I know, 1920! Of course the Flake has more recently become identified with its erotic advertising, but in fact it has *already* lasted over three quarters of a century.

Mrs Trevel (*smoking*)   Remarkable, isn't it!

Boulton   And here – (*Produces another package.*) the legendary Kit Kat, and it dates . . . ? (*Slight pause.*) from 1935! Yes the days of Hitler, and the airships, and the great ocean liners.

Mrs Trevel   I really love Kit Kat, I used to stuff myself with them while I was revising for my exams –

Boulton (*to* **Clare**)   You can have some, please, go on.

Clare (*smiles, nibbles a piece*)   Thank you. I'm not often offered sweets by parents, I can tell you!

Boulton   No? There's something almost perfect about the Kit Kat isn't there. To be controversial, it's almost Mozartian! Yes . . . And then of course there's Maltesers from 1936 . . . the ones with the less fattening centres. All these have lasted longer than most books of the period, most plays – I must *stress* this isn't about nostalgia, but I'm asking, as I expect you've guessed, is it possible to create classic confectionery, *now*, in present circumstances? Something that will endure?

Clare   So this is what really concerns you at your work? Is that what you're telling me?

Boulton   Just wait . . . wait one moment.

He produces out of his large bag, a collection of fresh vegetables.

I'll do this very quickly, I promise . . . I'd just like the chance
to show you, (*He smiles.*) don't get alarmed . . .

He is arranging the vegetables in front of her.

Mrs Trevel (*lightly, to* **Clare**)   You're going through a
phase of people *bringing* you things, aren't you! Firstly it's me
and my old newspapers, now it's vegetables.

Boulton   Yes. So – (*Having arranged vegetables.*) In our
efforts to relaunch the Meal in the Cup . . . to transform it.
And I don't think one could have a less fashionable product
to relaunch, could one? . . . The very bottom end of the
market, of Ready Cooked Meals . . .

Mrs Trevel   That is certainly true.

Boulton   So here's the array of vegetables that went into
our first mix, the prototype. Potatoes of course, tomatoes, all
the obvious, *plus* broccoli, *three* sorts of mushrooms, several
kinds of onions, courgette, aubergine and a really
imaginative idea – some JERUSALEM ARTICHOKES.
Though I say it myself, an inspired touch . . .

Mrs Trevel (*helpfully*)   They were trying to recreate a
strong farmhouse taste.

Boulton   That's right. (*To* **Clare**.)   I don't mind you
smiling –

Clare   No, I wasn't. I wasn't smiling.

Boulton (*smiles*)   I really don't mind . . .
So what happens, after we present our first mix? *This is what
they do.*
Not just for cost reasons – but because blandness is deemed
essential, OUT go the mushrooms, except for the dreary
button sort of course! Out go the courgettes, cut! Out go the
broccoli and aubergine, cut! And of course out go the
Jerusalem artichokes, *absolutely cut.*
The mix is reduced to something coarse and uninteresting,

and naturally now very closely resembles other products on the market.

He has tossed all the other vegetables back into bag leaving just three remaining.

I just want you to taste . . .

He has produced three mugs and is filling them with granules, and from a thermos hot water.

These are some of the remaining granules, of our first effort.

Clare   Like gold-dust now, I expect.

Boulton   Absolutely. (*Pouring hot water into mugs.*) You see I came prepared. It is hot I hope, but not too hot. Please drink.

Clare   Drink?

Boulton   Please — just a taste . . . to see the difference.

Clare   It's like the Pepsi challenge. (*She takes a small sip.*) Yes, that is nice, *genuinely* nice.

Mrs Trevel   That is good, yes. Really quite rich, pungent.

Clare   And this? — (*She tastes the other.*) Yes . . . the difference is very marked, pretty huge in fact. (*Genuine.*) That's a shame.

Boulton   We are unanimous then. (*To* **Mrs Trevel**.) If you could leave us now please, thank you.

Mrs Trevel (*as if she's been expecting this*)   Yes. Of course.

She exits. Silence. **Clare** *takes another sip, not knowing what* **Mr Boulton** *wants.*

Boulton (*smiles*)   I don't suppose you've had the tragedy of a Ready Cooked Meal demonstrated to you before . . . !

Clare   No. (*She smiles.*) That's certainly never happened before.

Boulton   I know it's something that you would never, ever think of buying yourself —

Clare   Don't be so sure, you haven't seen my cooking . . . !
Anyway I'll certainly walk around the supermarket with a
different perspective now, see the passion that is coming off
the shelves —

Boulton   I'm glad you said that. (*Slight pause.*) Because
being a bright person, you probably spotted what I'm about
to say.

Slight pause.

Clare (*watching him*)   I don't think so . . .

Boulton   When you and Leo are together here you *do* find it
comic, my work, don't you? Laugh together about it, I know
that's what goes on. Or went on.

Clare   No, Mr Boulton. That certainly did not go on here.

Boulton   I know that's what took place. I don't blame you
. . . but I *know*.

Clare   I can assure you, Leo and I do not sit around
laughing at your work. That is a total misconception, if I
may say so, of what goes on here. I do not spend my time, it
doesn't matter which child is in here, I do *not* discuss their
parents' work, of course I don't.

Boulton   Excuse me, but whether it was overt or not, I
know you DID. (*Serious, but not angry.*) *I know that's what went
on*. I can see . . .

Pause.

Clare   Well, if somehow, and I promise you it was
inadvertent, if somehow I gave that impression to Leo, then I
am truly sorry. But I don't see how that could have
happened, because it's not what I feel. (*Looking at him.*) The
idea of taking time, to make something better, and different
. . . not just settling for being like all the other products. Of
course I understand that.

Slight pause. **Boulton** *leaps up.*

Boulton   That will do. That is fine by me . . . ! And please,
keep the drink. (*He laughs.*) No, I would like you to!

He gathers his possessions together.

I'm pleased with Leo's progress . . . no doubt it will
continue.
And I know you don't need telling how much I care about
him. (*He moves.*)
And I'm glad to have had the chance to demonstrate
something – however eccentric it may have seemed. It was
important. At least to me.

He moves again.

Now I must get going – the car – the meter's running (*He
laughs.*) as usual, my fear of wardens!

Clare Mr Boulton –

Boulton No, it's fine. I am satisfied. That is all I wanted
from you. I needed to show you – and for you to say what you
did.

He moves to exit.

That's perfect.

He exits.

Clare *looks after him for a moment. She is affected by the encounter.
She smiles.*

Clare (*calls*) Gina . . . could you come in here please.

In the moment before **Gina** *enters,* **Clare** *sips the meal in a cup, again
struck by how good it is.*

Is Mrs Trevel still here – or has she gone?

Gina Oh yes, she's still here, very much so.

Clare Yes. (*Slight laugh.*) I thought that was hoping too
much. Could you ask her to step in then.

Gina Of course. Richard Mellinger is here, by the way.
His second rescheduled appointment.

Clare I know. (*She smiles.*) Don't worry, I'll only be a
moment doing this.

Gina (*quiet*) I wasn't worrying . . .

Gina *exits.* **Clare** *sweeps her desk clear of the remaining spilt granules.*

Mrs Trevel *enters, also holding the mug she got from* **Boulton**.

Mrs Trevel   He let me keep mine too! (*She takes a sip.*) And it really is rather good, isn't it – the Meal in a Cup that never was!

Mrs Trevel *sits in front of her.*

Clare   Yes . . . (*Staring straight at* **Mrs Trevel**.) I had no idea that you knew Mr Boulton.

Mrs Trevel   I don't. It was purely by accident.

Clare   By accident? Really?

Mrs Trevel   We happened to meet – mutual friends . . .

Clare   Now, I want to make myself extremely clear, Mrs Trevel. It would be a very bad move if you tried to go around stirring up the other parents, and it is not something I will tolerate.

Mrs Trevel   I'm not stirring anybody. (*She smiles, looking relaxed, summery.*) Although if I was, it's not clear how you would stop it. But that's another matter.

Clare (*very authoritative*)   Any grievance you have, any unfinished business, is with me. And should not involve anyone else.
If you *want to continue seeing me* – I advise you to listen to this.

Mrs Trevel   Oh, I see. (*She smiles.*) That's your sanction, is it? Good. (*She sips drink.*)

She smiles, relaxed.

But there's really no need for this. I happened to meet him and he told me what was on his mind, that he wanted to clarify the work he did, *to you*. And I said – because I did find his story genuinely interesting – I said I'd come and support him.

Because as you've just seen, it was difficult for him, it wasn't a very normal thing to do . . . (*Self-mocking laugh.*) Though as

you know that's not something I worry about myself! . . .
(*She smiles.*) I'm not exactly an authority on what's normal.

She smiles at **Clare**.

Come on, you can agree with that . . . !

Clare (*calmly*)　And Mr Boulton left reasonably content, I
think. So that's a further reason for him to be left in peace.

Mrs Trevel　You did very well with him, I'm sure. (*She
glances at office toy.*) You've got new office decorations, I see.

Clare　They're my father's, (*Slight smile.*) part of my
inheritance.

She looks at her.

Now – have you been to see any of the colleagues I suggested?
And has George found a new –

Mrs Trevel　Come on, now don't spoil it. (*She smiles.*) You
know I won't talk about that.

Clare　I would like to remind you that the last time you
were here, there was an incident, some violence –

Mrs Trevel　'Some violence' . . . ! Yes, don't worry, I
haven't forgotten. I've already said I'm sorry. (*She laughs.*)
Let's hope there's no need for me to say that again!

Clare　Mrs Trevel, I do urge you –

Mrs Trevel　Please, you've done your duty. I understand.
But do not tell me I need help, OK!

Raising her hand.

And before you say anything, I've actually come here with a
proposal. A compromise, because we don't want to turn into
Punch and Judy, do we? With me keeping on coming at you?

Clare (*watching her carefully*)　No . . .

Mrs Trevel (*smiles*)　And I must be quick, because that
gloriously handsome boy is waiting outside to see you . . . *So*
– if you give me just *some* of George's records, you can fillet

them, like the Government do to their files, you can sanitise them.
Just give me something – then I'll be satisfied.

Clare   I don't think that will be possible.

Mrs Trevel   We could get it all over today.

Gina *enters.*

Gina   Jess is on the line . . . Will you take it?

Clare   Jess? Yes. Absolutely. (*To* **Mrs Trevel**.) If you'll excuse me . . .

Mrs Trevel *gets up.*

Mrs Trevel   Right – shall I come back later to see if you've got anything to give me?

Clare   I don't think I will be here later –

Mrs Trevel   I'll try anyway, then we can all have a good bank holiday . . .

She exits.

Clare *takes the phone call.*

Clare   Yes. Jess? Where are you . . . ? By some gasworks . . . (*Sharp.*) King's Cross? . . . not King's Cross. Where then? . . . the Oval? . . . not there either. Well, I'm not going to spend my time playing guess the gasworks of London. (*Pause.*) So are you going to tell me where you are? . . . You're not. OK.

She sips mug.

No, I'm just drinking something. No, it's not coffee . . . no it's a little complicated. Yes . . . a complicated drink! (*She smiles.*) A farmhouse brew.

Calmly.

You're not coming on Tuesday? . . . why? You never usually ring up to cancel, you going somewhere? You're not. So why is this, Jess? No, I don't think we should move it to some other

time. You're not coming again this summer . . . I see. No . . .
I don't agree.

You'll think about it? . . . Good. Are you alone? No, I just
wondered. OK, call me later today. Yes . . .

Jess – you don't want to tell me anything else? You're sure?
Right.

She rings off.

Richard *has entered half-way through the conversation, he is dressed
in a smart suit, but he is carrying a large rucksack.*

Clare *stares for a second at the phone, deep in thought. Then looks up.*

Clare   Richard!

Richard   Sorry, I came in, didn't want to miss you.

Clare   That's all right. (*She smiles.*) You always look so
smart. What's all this luggage?

Richard   You've caught me on a day when I'm in transit.
(*Glancing over his shoulder.*) That woman was here again – I
didn't want her messing things up.

Clare   Don't worry, she's gone. I'm free.

Richard   But I want –

Gina *enters.*

Clare   Yes, Gina? Is something the matter?

Gina *hesitates. Unusually long pause.*

Gina   No . . . no.

She moves to door.

No, I'm sorry. It's nothing. (*She turns.*) By the way I've
decided I'd better stay – in case *she* comes back. (*She exits.*)

Richard   Look, I don't want you to say *no*.
I realise there's sort of unofficial rules for seeing ex-clients,
and this would be breaking them – but I want to go *outside*,
for this meeting. Don't say why.

Clare   Why? (*She smiles.*) I have to say why . . .

Richard   That Woman may come back for a start . . . ! I just want it to be less formal, I know I'm setting off all sorts of psychology beeps and bells . . . 'Why won't he stay here?' 'Why is it so important he moves out of here?'
But say yes . . . It's a lovely day out there . . . SAY YES!

Pause.

Clare (*considering*)   Well, I've got to get my car from under Marble Arch . . . maybe we can take a taxi over there . . . and then have a cup of coffee.

Richard   *Let's*! (*Smiles at* **Clare**, *as she hesitates*.) I could threaten I won't tell you anything unless we do!
Say yes . . . !

Blackout.

Scene Two

The Marble Arch standing upstage.

Marble Arch, the triumphant Arch is very recognisable, in a rough and vivid way, made out of cardboard, about four feet high. But it is covered in McDonald's logos, all over it. In a variety of sizes.
And arched over the top, like two cherubs, are two McDonald's clowns.

Hot strong sunlight, the sound of some music drifting from elsewhere in the park, bare stage apart from the Arch and one normal park rubbish bin.

Richard *and* **Clare** *enter.*
Richard *carrying his enormous rucksack.*

Richard   It's too hot for coffee . . . ! How about here? We'll sit in the sun.

Clare   I think we need a bench, don't we? I'm not really dressed for lying on the grass . . .

Richard   No, no, I have a surprise, wait! (*He grins.*) I have a solution.

He drops the rucksack on the ground, and begins slowly to open it.

Clare (*smiles*)   A solution? Sounds interesting . . .

Richard *as he teasingly slowly opens rucksack, glancing around.*

Richard   I used to love it round here as a kid. *Speakers Corner* that was great! Bet you find it interesting what goes on there with your line of work.

Clare   You mean all sorts of different obsessions on show? – Pouring out at full volume! . . . Yes.

She moves.

I remember a man screaming at the top of his voice, that the whole city should be colonised by tropical parrots! – Of course, I haven't been there for years.

Richard   Yeah . . . and there are all the luxury hotels and the cinema with one of the biggest screens in the city – used to dream away afternoons in there. (*He glances over his shoulder.*) At least the old Arch looks the same . . .

Clare   Yes – I suppose it does. (*She laughs.*) Sometimes, when I'm in certain moods – it looks different to me. (*Turning back, indicating rucksack.*) So come on, Richard! . . . What mysterious object is coming out of there?

Richard (*making a flourishing noise*)   Dee dah!

He produces a large quilt, out of the rucksack.

Here we are . . . let me spread it at your feet.

Clare   Do you always carry one around with you?

Richard   And so big. (*Grins.*) You've got to take a good look first – it will surprise you.

He holds up the big quilt. It is a mosaic of airline logos, cut off plastic airline bags, from all over the world, and carefully woven into a quilt. A patchwork of trans-world flying.

(*Smiles.*) So what do you think?

Clare   What do I think?

She pauses, staring at the quilt.

I think you must have clocked up a hell of a lot of air miles. Somehow.

Richard   Certainly. Yeah . . . ! (*He grins.*) So it did surprise you! These are all the airlines I have used – the Logos of the World. With a little cheating of course, here and there . . . I have to admit there are some I haven't used personally, but begged, or stole from people. (*He smiles.*) Or committed murder for.

Pause. He looks at **Clare**.

It's good, isn't it.

Clare (*quiet*)   It's great.

Richard   Step on it, go on . . . You see, you can trace some of my journeys.

Clare   Can I? (*She steps onto the quilt.*) So you really went from America to Africa . . . to Indonesia? Really, Richard? – then down to South America . . . ?

Richard   Yeah, pretty much! During gaps in the course. My girlfriend and I did this . . . the sewing . . . took us ages. And wait a minute.

Clare *about to sit.*

Richard   I want you to look carefully – because there are a couple of clues hidden there, clues to something *interesting* . . . I wonder if you can spot them . . . ?

Clare (*looking for a moment*)   No. (*Puzzled.*) I don't think so . . . do you mean clues to which countries you *really* went to?

Richard   No, no, better than that. (*He grins.*) You'll see it. OK, you can sit on it now. (*He is delving into rucksack.*) Here, is another smaller one!

He puts the small quilt next to the big one, but at a safe distance away from them.

In case we have company – somebody we don't want to get too close! Like that strange lady Mrs Trevel . . . in case she pops up!

Clare   Jesus, I hope not. Why do you say that?

Richard   Because whenever I see you (*He grins.*) she's always there.

He sits on the quilt, but initially there's a considerable distance between him and her.

Now – you've got to admit there couldn't possibly be anything better to sit on in the park, than this!

Clare (*smiles*)   I admit it. (*She looks at the logos.*) Maybe it'll take off of its own accord . . .

Richard *is gazing around him.*

Richard   One moment!

He leaps up, walks upstage, looks at the ground.

It's OK, I just thought I saw something . . .

Clare (*lightly*)   Don't say *you've* found something on the grass . . .

Richard   No. (*Grins coming back to join her.*) Not much of interest over there, just a couple of needles . . . not worth it!

He sits.

Now – just one other thing we desperately need . . .

He delves into the rucksack.

Clare (*laughs*)   Something else . . . coming out of there?

Richard *produces ghetto-blaster.*

Richard   We must have our ghetto-blaster, of course, can't do without that!

Clare   Do we really need that?

Richard   Absolutely! Got to noise pollute the atmosphere, it's essential . . . got to look as if we belong in the park.

He switches on ghetto-blaster.

There are some surprises on here too . . .

The ghetto-blaster begins to play — initially pleasant soft rock, lilting out.
He takes off his jacket, undoes his shirt slightly, beginning to sun himself.

Richard (*grins*) Now, we could be anywhere in the world!

Pause, he looks at **Clare**.

Tell me.

Clare Tell you what?

Richard Tell me, when other old kids come back to see you —

Clare Yes?

Richard How are they . . . ? How do they treat you?

Clare Well . . . Some of them don't look me in the eye. They smile, but they look everywhere except at me. Some kids seem to stoop, like they're trying to rediscover their original size, squeeze back into their old bodies — and others are very loud and confident . . . 'How are you, you old thing! Still at it!' Behave as if they're fifty-year-olds.

Slight pause.

Of course I don't see that many 'old kids', not after a gap of six years.

Richard (*moves slightly closer*) And what about the ones that were really special?

Clare 'Special' . . . ? (*Watching* **Richard** *closely.*) I can't afford to let any of them be really special.

Richard Can't you? (*Slight pause.*) Of course you can't.

Pause, he is staring at her.

What . . . if they became famous actors or something?

Clare (*lightly*) Well . . . I haven't been doing this long enough for that to happen. If you do it for thirty years — you may see children you knew become Top Politicians. And then each time you watch them on TV, all you can think of is them screaming at you 'you terrible, disgusting, evil, old bag!'

Richard   Yeah, I bet . . . (*Looking at her.*) that would be good! (*Slight pause.*) You know when I see somebody doing *your* job on TV or whatever, they *always* look like they've got a poker stuck up their arse – (*Turns to look at her.*) but you, you never do.

Clare (*laughs*)   Thanks, Richard!

Richard *leaning closer.*

Richard   What do you think I liked best about you . . . ? – you won't guess this – (*Slight pause.*) You never EVER used the word 'Skills', learning SKILLS, social SKILLS, lying SKILLS.

Clare (*laughing*)   Well, you were good at so many things, Richard.

Richard (*grins*)   Fuck 'Skills', I say.

Clare *watching him closely.*

The sound suddenly changes on the ghetto-blaster, the music stops, the sound of aircraft noise and nothing else, on the tape.

Clare (*startled looking at the ghetto-blaster*)   What's that? What's happened?

Richard   You've guessed, haven't you?

Clare   Guessed what?

Richard   About my time away. *You know.*

Slight pause.

Clare   Well, I know, maybe, it wasn't entirely happy.

Richard (*grins*)   You've guessed, that it was a nightmare, a disaster . . . a catastrophe.

Clare   Come on now, Richard –

Richard   No, no, it was interesting too! I spent a lot of my time in Airports . . .

Clare (*glancing across quilt*)   As I can see −

Richard   I called it Surfing the Terminals . . .

People are really nervous in airports not just from *fear of flying*, but they're setting out on a business trip that may change their life! Or a holiday which means a great deal to them, or you find them marooned because nobody has turned up to meet them −

Clare   And it's easy to get to know them . . . ?

Richard   Yeah! That's right, strike up an acquaintance! You know what's coming, don't you . . . ?
It's simple to get invited for a drink, or a HOLIDAY even!
. . . Get *Money*, of course . . . *Sex* − yeah − often . . .
Sometimes all those things in one hit!

And then on the plane it's easy to meet others − if necessary . . . see them struggling with their laptops, tap tapping away − suddenly not able to make them do what they want . . . you lean over, 'Can I be of help?' a look of such relief in their eyes . . .

I've done the airports of the world, Miss Attwood, I've seen many things.

Pause.

Clare   When did you leave the course, Richard?

Richard   I stuck it for five weeks − then I got the next flight out. And I tried to keep flying west − beat the clock.

I *have skills*, many skills of course, computing skills, all sorts, but there was nowhere I really wanted to land. *Nowhere*.

Clare   Well, Richard − I used to feel like that, at nineteen. I'm old enough to have been half a hippy, and done half the trail . . .

Richard (*loud*)   Don't give me that − don't you dare give me that!

Clare *very startled.*

Richard   Because *this is not the same*.

Clare   And why not?

Richard   Because – BECAUSE – everywhere I went, if it was on a plane, a little plane in South America, or if it was in an airport lounge, with those horrible metal tellies, they have, with those newsreaders that look exactly the same in each city of the world . . .
Absolutely everywhere I was – *I thought of you.*

I saw your face. I smelt you. I saw you.

Clare   Richard – you're exaggerating now, and you know it. You did *not* spend nearly six years thinking of me, that is not the truth.

Richard   Will you listen – I saw *you*, I saw your eyes, you looked at me from buses in New York, you looked at me from little cars in Mexico, I saw you.

He looks across at her.

And now you're this close . . .

He looks down.

You missed it, didn't you? – you see on the quilt . . . *the clues.* There is a 'C' and an 'A' there . . . (*Showing her on the quilt.*) and a whole 'Clare' there. You're all over here . . .

Clare (*looking down*)   Yes. But you could have put those there yesterday . . .

She suddenly looks up. A second later she abruptly gets up.

Jesus – what's the time?
Good God, it's twenty to four! Excuse me . . . (*She picks up her bag which is entangled in his legs.*) I *can't* have missed it!

She is pacing, scrabbling in her bag.

That's just not possible!

Richard   Missed what, what are you talking about?

Clare (*searching urgently through her bag*)   I've got to find the brochure – the programme with the times on . . . Where is it? Maybe he was on at 4.15 not 3.15.

She finds the programme tearing through the pages.

Make it 4.15 *please* . . . ! Where are we?

Clare   The Japanese . . . the Canadians . . . Martin
Pender – 15.15. 3.15! (*She moves.*) SHIT!

Richard   What was at 3.15?

Clare   A lecture. A very important presentation – my
partner is giving the most significant address of his career.

Richard   *And you missed it?* Well, you certainly can't have
wanted to be there!

Clare   No – that is not the explanation.
I thought there was more time – I thought it was later! (*She's
scrabbling in her bag again.*) Just got to make sure I've got the
ticket with me, for the conference, didn't leave it in the office.
It *is* extraordinary how it managed to slip my mind. I'll have
to work out how it happened . . . and *Gina* never said
anything.

She moves, searching for the ticket in her bag.

My car is under here, somewhere! In the car park. Right
under where we are luckily! If I've got my ticket, I can make
a dash across London, perhaps they're running late.

Richard   What will he do when he realises you weren't
there? Your partner? Will he be all understanding . . . or will
he pulverise you?

Clare   I've got the ticket! Thank God for that. (*She moves.*)
Right I've got to rush now . . . so we'll see each other another
time –

Richard (*catching hold of her*)   Oh no – you're not going!

Clare   Richard – let go – don't be ridiculous. Let go of me
at once.

Richard   You're not leaving yet.

Holding onto her.

You've broken one of your own rules, you came out with an old client, because you wanted to know the truth, and now you're going to hear it.

Clare   Richard, LET GO OF ME.

Richard *pulls her down onto the quilt, holding her very tight.*

Clare (*very formidable*)   You will let go of me at once, do you hear? Or I will be so angry with you, Richard –

Richard   You will, will you?

He is lying half on top of her, holding her powerfully.

You're alone in the park with me, anything can happen in parks these days. People vanish off the face of the earth – or get raped for hours, and nobody does anything, nobody answers their cries . . .

Clare *fighting back as he holds her.*

Clare   You're not frightening me one bit. You get off me – you're not going to hurt me and you know you're not. (*His face very close to hers.*) This is so unlike you, Richard –

Richard   You don't know what's 'like me'. You don't know what's happening to me any more.
And I *am* hurting you – because you felt you'd done so well with me, the success I was – your success . . . what you'd made me! I could see you glowing with it, your achievement, oh yes! I could see you, so pleased.

And *now*, you look at me. (*Pulling her head round, really hurting her.*) Look at what I'm like now . . .

Clare   You're making it impossible for me to do that. (*Her head being pulled back painfully.*) Stop this, control yourself, Richard. If you do stop it, we can have a proper time together, OK? Let go . . . will you? Let go.

Richard   You won't go? Promise. If I do. You'll stay?

Pause.

Clare   No. (*Slight pause.*) I won't go.

Richard *lessens his grip,* **Clare** *pushes free, she gets up.* **Clare** *is furious.*

Clare   Really, Richard! What was that for? What were you trying to show me?

Richard *sitting in the middle of the quilt.*

Richard   I know. (*Pause.*) That was stupid . . .

He looks across at her.

But don't go – please.

He begins to cry.

Shit . . . OK, this is obvious, this is an obvious thing to do . . . me crying . . . this isn't good either, but I *am* crying . . .

Clare *turns to look at him.*

Clare (*quiet*)   Richard . . .

Richard   Please, I need you here – just for now . . . (*Indicating all the logos.*) I'll take you on the journey I made – the whole one. Show you everything that happened.

Moving his hand across the quilt.

Here . . . and here . . .

Pause. He looks up at her.

But *please* don't go.

Blackout.

Scene Three

Gina *standing, tidying.* **Mrs Trevel** *smoking. Sound of rain outside.*

Mrs Trevel   I expect you want to be off?

Gina   I'm OK . . . don't worry about me.

Mrs Trevel   No – Gina, (*Smiles.*) I'm sure nobody has to worry about you.

Gina (*dryly*)   I try to make sure that's the case.

Mrs Trevel   And you do it really well!

She moves, casually.

You could always leave me here, if you wanted. I could mind the shop . . .

Gina   I don't think I'm allowed to do that.

Mrs Trevel   No . . . (*She smiles.*) Maybe you're right. Leaving me alone with the files on all the children and the parents – might be a wrong move! Yes . . . There's a chance I'd go tearing through them, while everybody was out . . . read all the secrets.

Mrs Trevel *laughs.*

Gina   What's the matter? What's funny?

Mrs Trevel   No, I was just thinking, I could ring round all the other parents 'come on over right now . . . find out what our kids really think of us . . . I've got the keys!' (*She giggles.*) Miss Attwood would come back, and find all these guilty looking couples, turning over her office.

Gina (*slight laugh*)   That wouldn't go down very well, no.

Pause. **Mrs Trevel** *looks at* **Gina**.

Mrs Trevel   I expect *you* hear a lot as the children wait out here, 'My mum thinks this', 'My dad won't let me do that!' . . . Heard anything particularly interesting recently?

Gina   I can't comment on that. You must realise.

Mrs Trevel   Yes, of course. (*Slight pause.*) Do you ever comment, Gina? On anything?

Gina   When I feel the need.

Mrs Trevel (*laughs*)   That's a marvellous gift to have, not to comment! I must take lessons from you, Gina – not commenting is something I find hard to do!

Martin *enters.*

Gina   Hello, Mr Pender.

Martin *doesn't react.*

Gina   Was it OK?

Mrs Trevel   Have you done your lecture?

Gina   Are you pleased? How did it go?

Martin   Fine . . . (*Moving around, very subdued.*) It went well, very well.

Gina   That's good, isn't it?

Mrs Trevel   Is Miss Attwood with you?

Martin   No – she isn't. (*Slight pause.*) I'm not sure she came.

Gina   She didn't go?!

Martin   She didn't attend, no. Not to my knowledge.

Mrs Trevel   Something must have come up.

Martin   Obviously –
It was a big success though. The jokes worked – and the image of this fat ungainly vehicle, bringing a whole city to a halt, *buggering* it up completely, that came across very clearly, I think.

Mrs Trevel   Good. I wish I'd heard it. It was something that needed to be said, and now it can't be contradicted.

Martin   Yes. And I did that. But . . . (*He pauses.*) But just after I finished, I discovered something. (*He stops.*)

Mrs Trevel   You discovered what?

Martin   No, it can wait.

Mrs Trevel   Tell me, I'm interested.

Martin   I discovered the most unexpected thing – a German academic came up to me, congratulated me, then said (*Momentary pause.*) HE'D just written a book about the METROBUS too. And it is to be published next week!

Mrs Trevel   A German . . . ! Written a book about the Metrobus?!

Gina   That's extraordinary.

Martin   It is! It's ridiculous! I said to him it's going to be published just in German, surely? And he said . . . 'Oh no, there's already an English translation, it comes out in *Britain* next week . . . Very good publisher!' (*He moves.*)
He said he'd written it to demonstrate how *not to do things* – for the Transport Planners of the World!

Mrs Trevel (*genuine*)   That is such bad luck . . . It must be really maddening for you.

Martin (*quiet*)   Maddening . . . I mustn't think like that (*He moves.*) I must try to stay calm . . . consider the implications.

Clare *enters. Her hair is slightly wet and rather untidy.*

Clare   Hello. (*Then seeing* **Mrs Trevel**.) Oh, and Mrs Trevel.

She moves over to **Martin**, *her mood preoccupied.*

I'm sorry, darling – something happened, I just *couldn't* be there.

Martin   You couldn't make it?

Clare   No.

Mrs Trevel   We'll withdraw. I think. That would be best. *I* can wait to be dealt with.

Clare (*half under her breath*)   I'm sure you can.

Mrs Trevel *turns at exit with* **Gina**.

Mrs Trevel (*to* **Clare**)   Are you all right?

Clare   All right . . . ? Yes. It's just raining out there. I walked, I didn't have an umbrella.

Mrs Trevel   You walked? Where from?

Clare *slight hesitation.*

Clare   From Marble Arch. I'm fine.

Mrs Trevel *and* **Gina** *exit.*

Clare (*touching* **Martin**)   I'm sorry, darling. There was a problem I had to deal with, somebody who used to come here.

Martin   Really? . . . (*Pause. He moves.*) Well, you missed something. It was great.

Clare   I'm sure – (*Affectionate.*) Did they make a recording of it? (*She smiles.*) Or can you do it again just for me – a private showing.

Martin   But there's something worse, worse than you missing it.

Clare   What?

Pause. **Martin** *paces, his anger erupting now he's alone with* **Clare**.

Martin   I have been beaten – BEATEN, by some fucking German academic, he's written a book too, on the same subject!

Clare   Does that matter?

Martin   OF COURSE IT MATTERS! You really think there's space for *two books* on the bloody METROBUS – of course there fucking isn't.

He paces absolutely furious.

I mean the bloody bus has been there since 1978, the fucking Leyland Titan. There could have been a book any time, but *nobody* thought to write it. And *now* suddenly there are two in the same fucking month! It's a disaster . . .

He moves.

I mean it would be incredibly funny if it happened to somebody else. (*He turns.*) Wouldn't it . . . ?
(*Pause, sarcastic laugh.*) I was such a fool – not to realise I should have written about the Trams of Frankfurt! I was crazy . . . !

Clare *watches.*

Clare   Martin, the work is what matters. *Remember* . . . ?

Martin   That's shit. What does that mean? (*Straight at her, very forcible.*) Tell me what that means? Come on.

Clare (*surprised by his tone*)   It means the work is good . . . and that'll be recognised, and anyway it's worth doing for it's own sake –

Martin   That is such *rubbish* . . . If I ever believed that, I don't now . . . ! It couldn't have been made any clearer could it – the true idiocy of that position – than it was today!

Clare (*startled*)   The idiocy . . . ?

Martin   Clare – I've just seen four years work go down the tubes – I've been whipped.
Timing is everything now – nothing else matters.
Nothing.
(*Loud, as he moves away.*) And don't tell me I'm wrong . . .

Pause, much quieter.

Jesus! I never expected this . . .

Clare   But the work is still there, it hasn't suddenly evaporated. That's not what's happened . . .

Martin   No?

Clare   The detail and the research are terrific. What does it matter if there's another book?

Martin   Stop saying that for Christ's sake. (*Slight pause.*) You know that idiotic woman out there was more sympathetic!

Clare (*quiet*)   I bet . . .

Martin (*suddenly*)   Get rid of her. She's always lurking around now, isn't she? Deal with her once and for all. Then we can talk . . .

Clare   Right, yes, that probably is best. Get her out of our lives.

Martin (*sharp*)   Or do you want me to – ?

Clare   No, no. I'll deal with it, (*She moves.*) it'll be settled.

Martin   I'm fetching her now . . . (*As he leaves.*) Make a job of it.

Clare *alone.*

Clare (*sharp*)   Make a job of it . . .

Mrs Trevel *enters.*

Mrs Trevel   Ready for me?

Slight pause.

Clare   I think so . . .

Mrs Trevel (*laughs*)   Nearly said something else, didn't you? (*Watching* **Clare**.)
You missed his lecture, your partner. How did that happen?

Clare   I had some unexpected business to attend to.

Mrs Trevel   I see. (*Lights cigarette.*) Right now, what's the agenda? – Get rid of the crazy lady? For good. Is that right?

Clare *looks up startled.*

Mrs Trevel (*smiles*)   You should be able to do that . . . easy.

Gina *enters with file.*

Gina   George Trevel's file.

Clare (*surprised*)   Gina, thank you – before I'd even asked for it!

Gina   Mrs Trevel suggested you might need it.

Clare   Right. (**Gina** *moving to go.*) No word from Jess?

Gina   No. (*She exits.*)

Clare *with George's file in front of her, opens it.*

Clare   So . . . you want something from here? One piece of paper – and you'll be satisfied?

Mrs Trevel   Yes.

Clare   Does that include this? – (*Holding up one sheet.*) Your son's birthday, height, weight and school?

Mrs Trevel   Maybe you could look just a little further.
(*Watching her carefully.*)
Are you allowed to use the word freaky?

Clare (*looking up startled*)   What?

Mrs Trevel   I had a young nanny looking after George,
everything was, (*She mimics.*) 'That's Freaky!' I supposed in
your job, you're not allowed to comment all the time 'That's
really freaky!' – Not very scientific.

Smiles, reaching in her bag.

Anyway I'm just warning you, you may find this really
freaky . . .

Clare   And what is in there?

Mrs Trevel   Aha, the other file – *My* File.
Don't look like that! (*She laughs.*) What's the ex-index
compiler up to now?

She produces piece of paper.

This is simple – you know broadsheet newspapers often run a
series of articles from members of the public, 'The Worst
Time of My Life' – that sort of thing? Well, there is a new
series – 'The Worst Experience with My Child'.
And *I've* done one – about you and I.
And my entry has been accepted. (*She lays it down in front of
her.*)
And it appears on Monday.

Clare *facing her.*

Clare   Is that a very wise thing to do, Mrs Trevel? Have
you had a lawyer look at it?

Mrs Trevel   All Names are Changed of course, as they
say.

Opening sheet of paper.

But here *you* are.

She looks up.

Who goes first? (*Without waiting for a reply.*) Me? OK . . .
'The first time I saw her, a handsome confident woman,
polite but formidable, and so very much in control – one of
the most self-possessed people I've ever met.'

Mrs Trevel *looks at* **Clare**.

Clare (*calmly*)   But she made you feel extremely lucky to be
allowed time with her – even though you were paying for it.
Is that what it says? Just guessing.

Mrs Trevel   I'm afraid it's not quite as tame as that.
'A fatal mixture of complacency and arrogance' – that's
what it says down here!

She looks up at **Clare**.

'As I moved nearer to her I realise we're about the same age.
Soon I work out we're both grammar school girls, both from
lower-middle-class families, though of course *she* assumes
I'm from a much posher background – both growing up in
unfashionable parts of London, glorious Acton and Hendon
respectively.' I like that bit . . .
'We probably both had our first sexual experiences about the
same time – maybe even shared the same taste in boyfriends,
tall gangling types, certainly we liked the same music . . .

Slight pause.

'*Now we couldn't be more different.*'

She looks up.

What does yours say?

Clare (*watching her very closely*)   It's not as colourful, I'm
afraid, it's cold and factual.

Mrs Trevel   Cold is good.

Clare (*staring at file*)   'George's mother is very determined
to get results . . . highly motivated for her child.'

Mrs Trevel   I love that, 'highly motivated'.

Clare   'Her previous employment shows up in a habit of
amassed random pieces of information.' (**Mrs Trevel**

clucking in agreement.) 'But currently she is unemployed, her main focus very much her home life –'

Mrs Trevel (*suddenly very animated*)   Why don't you say Housewife. I want to be that – officially. I'm proud to be an 'Ordinary Housewife', it's such a great phrase. You should dare to call me that. OK!

Slight pause.

Clare (*giving her a couple of pages*)   Here, have those. (*As* **Mrs Trevel** *looks at them.*) Mrs Trevel, did you write this article, and get it published, purely *for this moment*, so you can have a kind of 'duel'?

Mrs Trevel (*calmly*)   Yes. Do you want some fruit? (*She produces some peaches from her bag. Amused smile, glancing at pages.*) You're right, this is bland, isn't it? (*She looks up.*) And mine of course is going to appear in *print*, in black and white.

Perfectly calm.

You mustn't forget what my real purpose is in all this. It's *what happens to you* – remember?

Eating fruit for a moment.

Now shall we get to the really gritty bits?
'SHE is unmistakably a product of late sixties/early seventies liberalism . . .' No, this isn't it . . . here!
'Despite all her poise – and while paying lip service to the worries of a middle-class mum like myself – she can't disguise her basic *contempt*. It is masked, of course, but I can see it.'
'Her real passion is reserved solely for those poor children, the NHS cases she deals with, those lost disadvantaged souls. She approaches what she's doing for *me* as purely a form of car maintenance – just tuning up the kids. Something that has to be endured, to pay for her real work.'

Pause. **Clare** *moves around stage taking cigarette out of* **Mrs Trevel***'s packet.*

Clare   That is ridiculous and simplistic.
I could say, quite calmly, I refute it.

But in fact it's utter shit, *total shit* and that's what it should be called.

Momentary pause. **Mrs Trevel** *watching*.

I clearly wouldn't survive a week in my practice if people thought that about me.
I do not make those judgements.

She moves over to cupboard in wall, begins to produce a series of Jess's models, both small ones and medium ones.

But there's something much more important that you're wrong about. Far more important *to me*.

She tugs at cigarette for a moment, the models in a pile at her feet.

Mrs Trevel   I didn't know you smoked.

Clare   I don't smoke.

She blows smoke.

I see children — all the time —

Mrs Trevel   Of course. I know —

Clare   — from all sorts of backgrounds. The children of famous novelists and members of the SAS, children of taxi drivers, of traffic wardens with their peculiar new uniforms, and one kid whose father is a pest controller.

She moves.

I have to get to know them, and especially their inner worlds. Have to be able to enter their imaginations — see the world through their eyes . . .
And what you said is *totally untrue*. It's garbage.

Mrs Trevel   Which particular piece of garbage of mine did you have in mind?

Clare   The story about George — when he asked you, 'Am I being targeted correctly, Mummy, towards the right market?' That is *not* how kids see themselves, or see the world now, none of them, not even your son. They do not feel there's such a *rush*.
That is an adult fantasy — a myth.

Mrs Trevel   That's what you're calling it?

Clare   *Yes*. Just like that other myth – that KIDS CAN'T CONCENTRATE any more, only for a couple of minutes at a time, because of TV, MTV, computer games . . . everything has to be images, and flicking channels, that is *such a lie* too!

Mrs Trevel   You *want* to believe it's a lie –

Clare   *No* – that is not what I find. From the kids. It's not what happens here. And yet it gets recycled again and again – 'books will be dead within five years' – it's absolute crap.

Mrs Trevel (*smoking*)   So I'm recycling myths, am I?

Clare   Kids' imaginations are just as vivid, just as anarchic, as ever, maybe more. (*Indicating models.*) Look at these, the work of a thirteen-year-old girl.

She stands them up across stage.

She started with a fragment of the Houses of Parliament, then she moved on to this great version of the Albert Hall! . . . a sort of super biscuit tin, whose top rolls off – with these strange rather sinister black lozenges inside – Christ knows what those are meant to be!
The whole city is here – though there's a particular bias towards South Kensington for some reason!
Harrods oozing as you can see . . . a very spiky, dangerous Albert Memorial . . .

Mrs Trevel *moving among models.*

Clare   Just think of the amount of time and concentration that's gone into these! Hours and hours, to create her vision of the city.

Mrs Trevel   They're great. Strange . . . but great. You should open it to the public, a model city on your roof! (*She looks up.*) You must find her a really interesting case.

Clare   Yes, she is, I'll admit that. She does all this work for me, but she will do nothing at school.

Mrs Trevel   This is Jess?

Clare   Yes.

Mrs Trevel   The one you're waiting to hear from? I can see why.

She kneels down centre stage, among the models, to look at them more closely.

They're haunting – a sort of two-finger salute, a fuck-you sign, to anybody who looks at them. (**Clare** *turning in surprise.*) And here's the American influence . . . how we half embrace it and half hate it. And they all look uninhabited, don't they?

Picks one up.

Is this what's happening to the city? Nobody knows what the centre of cities will look like, do they? – when everybody's work patterns change.
Somebody said, on the radio, 'Oh, the inner cities will be regenerated by the Entertainment Industry!' What crap that is!

Clare   Yes, that is.

Mrs Trevel   I'd like to keep one of these, a very small one, maybe Battersea Power Station. (*She is kneeling among them.*) God preserve me, from *my* children being too *original*.

Clare   What? (*Sharp.*) What did you say?

Mrs Trevel   I said, don't let my children be too original please – they'll never succeed.

Clare   You really think that?

Mrs Trevel   Yes.

Clare   That's a startling thing to say . . . (*Slight pause.*) Never heard somebody say that.

Mrs Trevel *gets up.*

Mrs Trevel   It's really raining now . . . (*Suddenly turning.*) Do I get to hear my child's recording – what he said here?

Clare   No, you do not.

Mrs Trevel   So there *is a* recording? Of George?

Clare   Maybe.

Mrs Trevel (*watching* **Clare**)   What happened at Marble Arch? Something happened to stop you getting to the lecture?

Clare   A boy, who used to come here, got overexcited.

Mrs Trevel   He attacked you?

Pause.

Clare   No, not attacked, no. That's overstating it. He got upset.

Mrs Trevel   Was it that beautiful boy who's always waiting to see you?

Clare   I'm not commenting on that.

Mrs Trevel   It obviously was.

Clare   I told you –

Mrs Trevel   It must have been unpleasant, whoever the boy was. Suddenly all this bile coming out – was it bile? It must have been a shock. (*Slight pause.*) Come on, you can tell me – before they come in . . . Did he bruise you? (*Taking her arm to look,* **Clare** *flinching.*) Jesus . . . ! You're really hurt.

Clare (*obviously in pain*)   No. It's nothing. (*Slight smile.*) You get very used to kids hurling abuse at you in this job. It happens quite a lot.
(*Quiet.*) I just wanted . . . I suspected this individual was not as happy as he made out . . . but I wanted him to be . . . I wanted to be proved wrong.

Pause.

But it was OK. I'm fine . . .

Mrs Trevel   You walked across London in the rain. Even though you were late for everything! And you say it's OK?

Clare Yes. What's more my car was parked right underneath where we were, right below, and yet I walked all the way back.
That must seem a little odd, I admit.

Slight pause. **Clare** *has turned away.*

Mrs Trevel I'll take you back there. To where your car is. I'll give you a lift.

Clare No. That's not necessary.

Mrs Trevel Oh yes, it's easy for me. On my way. We'll go there together.

Clare Thank you, but no –

Mrs Trevel I think you should come.

Clare You can have this. (*Handing rest of file.*) The whole file – I really don't see why not now.

Mrs Trevel *takes file, but doesn't bother to look at it.*

Clare Have you got what you wanted?

Mrs Trevel No. You were right – it's not going to be of any interest to me. (*Looking across.*) That's why you should come.

Gina *enters.*

Clare (*sharp*) Yes, Gina?

Gina (*glancing from one to another*) I just wondered if you needed anything . . . ?

Mrs Trevel Been hovering outside? Don't worry, she's still in one piece.

Clare It's OK, Gina.

Gina Yes . . . (*Glancing at Jess's models.*)

Mrs Trevel We've made a little bit of mess – but you'll forgive that I'm sure. (*She smiles indicating models.*) I don't know yet if I'm going to be allowed to keep one of these or not? You never guessed you might be able to buy me off that way . . . !

She moves.

I'll just get the car . . . OK? Don't worry I've got a mighty umbrella, I'm fine! I'll park right outside, dash in and get you.

Gina   Get who?

Mrs Trevel   Miss Attwood. (*As she exits.*) I'm leaving the front door on the latch . . . that's safe, isn't it?

Mrs Trevel *leaves.* **Gina** *watching her go, apprehensively. She turns.*

Gina   Where are you going with her?

Clare   She's just giving me a lift – back to where I left my car.

Gina *hesitates, doubtful.*

Gina   Right . . .

Clare   Gina? Tell me. (*Pause.*) Tell me what's on your mind.

Gina   No . . . It's OK. It's nothing.

Clare *angry, then restraining herself.*

Pause.

Clare   Is it my imagination – is it paranoia, not something I usually suffer from – or did you remember about Martin's lecture, when I was about to go out with Richard? You guessed that I might have got the time wrong. You came in – and then deliberately didn't remind me.

She looks at **Gina**.

I'm right, aren't I?

Gina   I didn't want to interfere.

Clare   What?

Gina   I wasn't going to interfere.

Clare   WHAT? Come on, Gina! For once, *just once*, give it to me.

Gina (*comes bursting out with it*)   All right — for once — if you want me to!
It is because I don't understand.

You don't do things how *I* would. Like . . . like . . . I mean, parents say to you 'I want my child to come twice a week for the next couple of months, and after that only once a week because life's busier then.'
And *you* say to them, '*No no* I can't agree to that . . . *I* decide when he comes, and how many times . . .'

You're giving a service! You *have* to provide a *service*.

If they want your mobile number, then for God's sake you give it to them!
Because if you don't, they're sure going to go and find somebody doing your job who will. (*Watching her.*)
You CAN'T disagree with them. *You can't do it like that!* But you don't seem to have realised!

Clare (*pause*)   Thank you, Gina. (*Slight smile.*) I was right then to feel a chill of disapproval coming from you.

Gina   And today — OK, you want to hear about today?! And so I thought, I mustn't intervene. Miss Attwood has her own agenda. I must let it take its course. She has her own way of doing things. *That's what happened*!

Clare   Sounds like bullshit to me, Gina. You thought — I'm going to move on to another job soon, so just let's step back and watch how things unfold here — see if she comes a cropper.

Gina   You think it's *bullshit* . . .
OK! And that's true of my whole attitude . . . ?! And you think you're gloriously free of bullshit, don't you! Well, maybe you are . . . (*Staring at* **Clare**, *very calm.*) But I know what's necessary for me . . .

Martin *enters.*

Martin   She's gone! She HAS gone!

Gina   Mr Pender, I think I'm about to be fired . . .

Martin   *Fired*? Why should anybody fire you? Clare, you're not going to, are you?

Gina   Yes. Because she missed your lecture.

Martin   That's no reason for firing anyone . . . !

He moves.

I have a plan now anyway, I've moved on to the next stage . . .
I've been thinking about it out there – it's obvious! I have to discredit and destroy the German's book . . . *undermine* it . . . There's no way it will be as thorough as mine. I hope! I have to go on the offensive.

Gina   That's right. I'm sure that's right. Go for it!

Martin   Blow it out of the water! (*He smiles.*) If you *can* blow buses out of the water . . .

Gina   I bet you can!

Martin   Have to move quickly, shiftily. (*Sharp grin.*)
Maybe even get to review it, the German's book, give it a stinker. If I do nothing, obviously, I have lost completely. I've got to make a virtue out of the timing – two books, one of which is shit, one of which is good. I've got to hound him. *Finish* him. (*To* **Clare**.) What do you think?

Clare   It's not your normal, calm way of solving things. Does it have to be that brutal?

Martin   Yes, I think so. Now it has. (*Slight pause.*) Even the world of the old Metrobus has to be brutal . . .

He smiles to himself.

That is the only way . . .

Pulls out notebook, moves, beginning to write.

I just need to make a couple of notes, while these ideas are still fresh . . .

Pause.

Gina   Mrs Trevel is taking Clare off somewhere.

Clare (*turning, looking at* **Gina**)   You've never called me that before.

Martin (*writing in notebook*)   What, where to?

Clare   It's OK – it's just a ride to my car.

Martin   Why? – You know she's a rather unbalanced woman, to put it mildly! (*He is writing in his notebook, only half attending.*) You can't trust her at all . . . she wants to cause trouble for you, make you do something – she's trying to provoke you.

Clare   Clearly.

Pause. **Martin** *concentrating on his notes.* **Clare** *moves, picking things up putting them in her bag.* **Martin** *looks up.*

Martin   What you doing?

Clare   Just collecting a few things – it's the only way to see her off.

Martin (*watching things go into her bag*)   Your father's ancient office toys! I don't understand.

Gina   Don't go with her, it's not a good idea.

Martin (*deep in his notes again*)   Get a cab . . . When I finish . . . I've just got a few more thoughts to get down – I'll come with you . . .

Clare   No, I *want* to do this.

Martin *looks up, very surprised.*

Martin   Clare, I leave you alone with her, to get *rid* of her and look what happens! Suddenly you're accepting lifts with her! (*Returning to his notes, he has to complete them.*) And *don't* tell me 'you know what you're doing'.

Clare   Right. OK, I won't.

She smiles.

Actually, I probably don't.

Mrs Trevel *enters. They look at her.*

Mrs Trevel   Ready? Coming?

Blackout.

Scene Four

Clare *standing centre stage, shaking a bottle of pills.*

Clare   Leo, on drugs . . .

(*As Leo.*) Sure I've taken a few, Ecstasy, I take that like
vitamins. Yeah . . . means nothing to me . . .
So common at my school, they've got a slot machine for it –
you walk in, put in fifty pee, out it comes, one tablet. And it
helps! Oh yeah . . . *You* try getting through a day at my
school without it!

Clare   George on drugs . . .

(*As George.*) I find them on the pavement, people miss them
completely! But I see them and they're lying there, for free! I
collect them, keep them on the window-sill. Next to my
money. But I don't take them.

She puts on coat.

Clare   Jess . . .

(*As Jess.*) I don't use 'em. Not much. You don't believe me –?
I shot up a couple of times. But I don't need them. Mind you,
it's better than sex . . .

This boy is rubbing me, big sloppy kisses, suddenly he's
between my legs, really rough. Then he turns me round –
pushes me against the wall – he can't really do it from behind
– he's just clumsy. But my nose is stuck against this poster –
and you know what it's for? It's for a fucking lottery. *Not* the
National Lottery, that wouldn't be too bad! – But this was
ANOTHER LOTTERY – for a bloody garden centre!

Then I'm walking away, really slow and sore, and I'm
thinking why don't I start Jess's Official London Walks?!

You know like the Dickens Walks, and the Sherlock Holmes Walks . . . and while I'm thinking this I suddenly take off — no drugs I promise, this *wasn't drugs.*

I'm in the air. I'm like a hang-glider, I'm floating across the roofs of London, I see a film star down there on her roof kissing her dog . . . I see a stand-up comic with his roof-top pool — incredible blue water, with a sunken sculpture in it . . .

And then right below me there's some professional villains, in their big roof-garden, yeah, with among the flowers they've got a mock-up of a security van! — So they can have practice armed raids — while they're sunbathing!

I'm going across all of this.
Past my window, where I live . . . with the mashed potato still on the screen, on those buttocks, except it's going a bit black from all the smoke.

I'm not *stopping* . . . I'm away . . . I'm right away. Away from school. Away from you. You're not going to get me back. YOU'LL NEVER GET ME BACK.

Clare *exits.*

Light changes.

Marble Arch.

The model of Marble Arch turned round so we see its reversed side. The other side of the model is covered in thick dark bristles, with pieces of litter and flotsam caught in it.

Glowing fluorescence along the back wall. And pieces of long metal strands — fragments of an old machine down stage.

Mrs Trevel *enters.*

Mrs Trevel   Come on, I'm sure it's this way.

Clare *enters carrying bag.*

Clare   I told you we shouldn't come down that walkway. I have *never* been lost before trying to get into an underground car park!

Mrs Trevel   We're not lost.

Clare   Oh no? Look at this . . . (*Dusty small metal notice on the back wall with an arrow.*) A pathetic little sign pointing to where the old car pound used to be . . . it's a genuinely scary part of the city, isn't it . . .

We're heading straight for some deserted tunnels! We'll find ourselves wandering deeper and deeper in to the bowels of Marble Arch . . .

Mrs Trevel (*glancing around*)   There's so much space down here, isn't there? Much more than anybody realises. We're right under where people used to be hung, Tyburn . . .

She looks up.

Murderers, highwaymen, dangling . . . where all the public executions took place.

Clare (*nervous laugh*)   Right, well! – On that note, I think I'll find my own way out. Do without you as a guide, thank you!

Mrs Trevel   You think you can just leave, like that?

Clare   Yes. With any luck.

Mrs Trevel   So why didn't you run off before? When we got out of the car? You had the chance . . .

Clare   Because I didn't realise you would insist on escorting me down here.

Mrs Trevel (*slight laugh*)   Come on, you knew you wouldn't be able to get rid of me that easily.

Quiet, watching **Clare**.

So you've decided – for some reason – to gamble on giving me a little more of your time?

Clare   Yes, well, I didn't plan to be alone with you in a subterranean –

She stops by the metal on the ground.

Shit . . . what is this?

Mrs Trevel   Oh, it's only some junk.

Clare   No. *No*, it's not junk.

She bends over it.

It's still recognisable. Just. It's the corpse of a photo booth –
the Automatic Photo Machine. It probably dates from the
sixties when this entire great hole was dug, and all the hotels
were built –

She squats close to the machine.

Yes . . . look, there's even a coil of photos . . . all smudged,
too black to see.

She stares close at innards of machine.

That's so funny –

Mrs Trevel   Funny, why is it funny?

Clare   Because today . . . because of my father's 'effects'
. . . I was thinking of my teenage years. (*She is fascinated by the
remains.*)

Mrs Trevel   *I* used to play in those when I was a kid,
taking photos of myself, making idiotic faces.

Clare   That's right . . . !
I would pile in with my friends, taking delicious,
'sophisticated' photos, with hats . . . ! Or rude *rude* pictures!
Used to go necking inside these – with some spotty boy, the
flash going off! Even had sex in them. Did you do that? (*Looks
across at her.*) No, maybe not . . .

She lifts part of the metal.

They seemed so new and exciting these machines, when they
first hit the streets, *so complicated!* . . . (*She laughs.*) The last
word in elaborate technology.
Now it's old and primitive.

Pause. She stares at it.

If there's *one thing*, that is so different, between now and then
– the city seemed REALLY CLEAN. It was very sexy, it was

erotic to come down to the West End, but it never seemed remotely dangerous.

The *wider* world was dangerous . . . Russia, Red Square, men in furry hats . . . but *not the city*.

Slight pause. She stares down.

This is a wonderful relic . . .

Mrs Trevel   You see, it *was a lie*.

Clare *turns*.

Mrs Trevel   You *did lie* to me – when you said you didn't long for the past . . .

Clare   I do *not* long for the past. (*Slight pause.*) You attacked me FOR THAT!?

She moves.

Is that what's going to happen again?

Mrs Trevel   Why would it happen again?

Clare   I don't know! I keep thinking that's what you're planning to do. Give me some sort of ritual beating. A new way of settling things with professionals that have let you down! Stuff litigation, let's go and beat the shit out of them . . . ! *Pulp them.*

Mrs Trevel   You came with me expecting to be beaten up? You really think that's what I'm after?

Clare   I'm not sure . . . But I can think of better places for it to happen!

Pause.

Let's see anyway –

She takes a small compact tape-recorder out of her bag.

What result this has –

Mrs Trevel   The tapes of George? Is that what you've got? So you're going to let me hear them after all.

Clare   If people came upon us now, two mature, 'well-dressed women' as they say in crime reports, playing tapes by a decaying photo booth . . . !

Mrs Trevel   To hell with that – play it.

Tape-recorder between them on the ground. **Mrs Trevel** *circling round it.*

Clare   There is a little of Leo first. Mr Boulton's boy.

We hear real kids' voices. **Leo's voice** *first, a high little eleven-year-old. But it is extremely intense, loud, very upset.*

Leo's voice   I don't want . . . I don't want . . . I don't want, I DON'T WANT TO STAY AT SCHOOL. (*He begins to stretch the words out so they have an insistent beat.*) No point . . . *no point don't want* . . . no point.

The tape changes.

Mrs Trevel   There's George – !

George's voice *pipes up boyish middle-class private-school voice.*

George's voice   MY DAD says he's like a monkey with a computer – and he says I'm like an ANGEL with a computer. Well, fuck that . . . ! . . . Do I want to be an angel with a computer? *What am I doing it for?*

He suddenly shouts desperately.

Nobody will tell me! . . . Nobody can tell me . . . Nobody CAN GIVE ME AN ANSWER.

Clare (*trying to reassure*)   A lot of shouting happens in sessions, with many different children. It's not unusual.

Mrs Trevel *listening with her back to* **Clare**. *She is fascinated. She does not seem bothered by the shouting. She seems almost excited.*

Mrs Trevel   Yes. (*Pause. She listens.*) Don't turn it down, turn it, up yes. Go on, turn it up.

George's *shouting is louder, intense.* **Mrs Trevel** *smoking, moving across stage.* **Clare** *is startled by her reaction,* **Mrs Trevel** *turns towards her.*

Clare   What are you smiling for? I was expecting you might get really angry, when you heard this – upset . . .

Mrs Trevel   No. This is OK . . . I need to hear this. (*As the little boy's voice continues to shout.*) This is all right.

Suddenly the tape changes to a girl's voice.

Clare   And this is Jess –

Mrs Trevel   No, don't stop it!

Jess's voice   So I bring these, *to you*. And you know what they're saying? All these models? – what they're 'expressing', that's what you want to know what they're really really saying – well, *it's this*!

She lets out a high-pitched noise, much stranger than the other children that builds from a hushed sound to a full scream.

Mrs Trevel (*quiet*)   Christ – it sends a shiver down one . . .

The noise again.

You failed utterly with her, didn't you.

Clare *suddenly switches off the tape. She turns sharply towards* **Mrs Trevel**. *She is furious.*

Clare   Thank you . . . thank you very much for that! (*Enraged.*) JESUS . . . !

For one moment she moves towards **Mrs Trevel** *as if about to hit her. She moves around her.*

I know you're trying to provoke me. 'Berserk Attack on Loving Parent' – good late addition for your newspaper article! And get me hounded out of the profession.

She moves clenched, around **Mrs Trevel**. *Resisting. Trying to stop herself hitting her. After a moment, slight smile.*

Instead maybe I will beat up an ex photo booth . . .

She stops moving. She kneels by tape-recorder. She lights cigarette. Her manner still clenched.

Mrs Trevel   Keep playing that girl. (*She turns.*) Please. *Please do it.*

Clare *switches on tape-recorder.*
Jess *is making a weird chanting sound, no longer a full shout, sometimes it sounds likes she's crying other moments something stronger, but it is deeply unsettling.* **Clare** *mouths to the sound for a moment.*

Clare (*quiet*)   Oh, Jess . . .

She stares at the sound.

OK OK.

She shakes slightly for a moment, by machine. Silence except for **Jess's voice**. **Mrs Trevel** *watching.* **Clare** *clenched up, crouched. Then she stops* **Jess**.

All right. You have got to me. (*Slight nervous laugh.*) Brought me to my knees – as you can see! If only for a moment.

You came after me, pushed and pushed.
When you were being blatant and threatening earlier on, it had very little effect at all.

She looks across at **Mrs Trevel**.

But today – for some reason – you have broken through. It's very strange, I don't know why . . . but it's like the professional mask I have to wear is not operating, people can see inside me – see exactly what I'm really thinking . . .
(*Pause.*) I've become transparent . . . cannot conceal . . .
The funny little father with his pot noodle . . . Richard – *you*.
That's what you've done. I hope it's not a permanent state.

Pause.

It's like I'm made of glass.

Mrs Trevel   Push hard enough and things happen.

Clare   Jesus – I wouldn't like to be you.

Mrs Trevel   Thank you –

Clare   But in many ways you're right.
Not, certainly not, about me making crude judgements about cases. And you're a Luddite, a romantic and a reactionary about the past . . . but despite – despite . . .

Mrs Trevel   Being crazy?

Clare   No, you're *not* crazy – immensely difficult to handle – a pain in the arse – but not crazy.

Mrs Trevel   I'm not crazy – that's official! (*Staring at* **Clare**.) I think I've got less conventional as I've grown older. Which is interesting . . . And I think I prove that it's possible to be at home all the time, and still *work out what's going on*.

Clare   That terrible remark you made about children not being too original, in a sense that's true . . .

Mrs Trevel   Yes. I know. And I'm right about the world spinning away from us.

Mrs Trevel *switches on* **Jess** *again*.

Clare   Yes . . . (*A particularly haunting sound from* **Jess**.) Shit – (*Quiet*.) What a noise . . .

She turns down the sound of **Jess's voice**.

You're right about a lot of the control, the Professional Control, in many areas, *being fake*.

Jess's *sound continues*. **Clare** *squatting beside it*.

Clare   I am here . . . surrounded by these kids' voices . . . and I'm saying to you – I don't know . . . I DO NOT KNOW.

Jess's voice, *her affecting cries, suddenly interrupted by* **George**, *and then* **Leo**. **George** *crying out 'what is there for me?' A blend of agitated nervous children's voices. The full power of their voices*.

Clare   Nobody knows what the fuck's going to happen. Because it's all changing so fast. People want service and solutions so quickly.

The children's voices running on.

I am already out of date, according to my own secretary!

Mrs Trevel *turns*.

Mrs Trevel   Panic is good.

Clare   What!?

Mrs Trevel   Panic is healthy . . . Panic is good.

Clare   You mean instead of 'Greed is Good' – 'Panic is Good'. Not sure it'll catch on somehow.

Mrs Trevel   Yes . . . Panic is right. The only intelligent reaction . . .

Pause. **Jess's voice,** *the children's voices.*

They can smell *our panic.* The kids.
But they can see we're pretending it's not there at all. (*Pause.*) That's why George ran away.

Clare   Perhaps . . . He watched very carefully what was going on . . . it is true. (*She laughs quietly.*) If I go round mouthing 'Panic is good', I'll have no clients left within a week. And *Jess* has already gone.

Pause. She smokes.

But maybe they are waiting for us to admit our ignorance. The kids . . . to hear us say we haven't the *faintest idea* how their lives are going to turn out. (*The sound of the children's voices.*) What work will look like . . . what *anything* will look like . . .

Sound of great clang, like metal exits being locked shut.

Clare   Shit – what on earth was that?

Mrs Trevel   Do they close this place?

Clare   They can't close all the exits, can they? We can't be shut in!

Pause.

Mrs Trevel   Got your mobile?

Clare (*laughs for a moment*)   No, I got rid of it.

Mrs Trevel   Wouldn't work down here anyway.

She starts getting things out of her bag, drinks etc.

Don't worry, we'll get out. (*Pause.*) The whole city's moving out there, the bank holiday. And here we are.

Clare (*stretching out*)   People will come, in the rush hour on Tuesday morning to use the car park and pick their way over these two barking looking women, their hair gone white by then probably!

We hear the children's voices again for a moment, a frightening startled sound, then they are quieter.

And I'll emerge up there, in the daylight, to find Gina running my practice probably! And Martin having murdered a German academic! . . . (*She smiles*) If my 'partner' and I ever split up it will be a problem, because I'll be reminded of him each time a bus goes past . . .

Pause.

'Deeply convenient' – that was how you described my relationship, that was a very *lucky* strike, wasn't it? – An accident . . .

Mrs Trevel   You reckon?

Clare   *Yes*. And if it *is* 'deeply convenient', it is probably what I need. (*She smokes, smiles.*) No doubt, the reality is in fact, that Martin and Gina understand the times perfectly – and it is *me* that is hopelessly out of touch!

Pause. She stares up.

By the time we get out . . .

Pause.

Maybe the whole world will have changed *again*, in *one weekend*. New cars . . . new money . . .

Sound of distant guitar strumming music echoing towards them through subterranean space.

Clare   Fuck, what is that now?

Mrs Trevel   The only other person down here.

Clare   A ghostly busker! That would make my day complete, being raped by a demented busker.

Mrs Trevel I think we can see him off, don't you!

Clare Yes . . . I suppose we'd seem a pretty terrifying duo.

The sound wafts away. **Mrs Trevel** *has assembled fruit, drinks, etc. from her bag.*

Mrs Trevel I'm making a little 'nest' here, we can have a picnic . . . we can last out if necessary!
When they found George – in the woods – at last – he'd built himself a rather strange hideaway . . . (*She laughs.*) maybe this is a subconscious copy.

Clare (*watching her*) And then you'll let me go . . . ?

Mrs Trevel You're free to walk away any time.

Clare You know what I mean.

Mrs Trevel I've already let you go . . .

She glances across.

Play Jess . . . she may not be making such a terrible racket now . . .

We'll let the city get away, let them sit in their three-mile tailbacks above our heads.

Jess's voice. *A softer singing sound. Still unsettling, but less harsh.*
Clare *listens for a moment.*

Clare I didn't know this was here. This sound. It's new, she must have played with the tape when I was out of the room . . . (*She blows smoke.*) I don't smoke . . .

Pause.

I'll have to listen to all my tapes again.

Mrs Trevel Yes, you will.

Clare See what's hidden on them.

She smokes; her tone calm.

And then Panic . . .

Fade.

Methuen Modern Plays

include work by

Jean Anouilh
John Arden
Margaretta D'Arcy
Peter Barnes
Sebastian Barry
Brendan Behan
Edward Bond
Bertolt Brecht
Howard Brenton
Simon Burke
Jim Cartwright
Caryl Churchill
Noël Coward
Sarah Daniels
Nick Dear
Shelagh Delaney
David Edgar
Dario Fo
Michael Frayn
John Godber
Paul Godfrey
John Guare
Peter Handke
Jonathan Harvey
Iain Heggie
Declan Hughes
Terry Johnson
Barrie Keeffe
Stephen Lowe
Doug Lucie

John McGrath
David Mamet
Patrick Marber
Arthur Miller
Mtwa, Ngema & Simon
Tom Murphy
Phyllis Nagy
Peter Nichols
Joseph O'Connor
Joe Orton
Louise Page
Joe Penhall
Luigi Pirandello
Stephen Poliakoff
Franca Rame
Philip Ridley
Reginald Rose
David Rudkin
Willy Russell
Jean-Paul Sartre
Sam Shepard
Wole Soyinka
C. P. Taylor
Theatre de Complicite
Theatre Workshop
Sue Townsend
Judy Upton
Timberlake Wertenbaker
Victoria Wood

Methuen World Classics

Aeschylus (two volumes)
Jean Anouilh
John Arden (two volumes)
Arden & D'Arcy
Aristophanes (two volumes)
Aristophanes & Menander
Brendan Behan
Aphra Behn
Edward Bond (four volumes)
Bertolt Brecht
   (five volumes)
Büchner
Bulgakov
Calderón
Anton Chekhov
Noël Coward (five volumes)
Sarah Daniels (two volumes)
Eduardo De Filippo
David Edgar (three volumes)
Euripides (three volumes)
Dario Fo (two volumes)
Michael Frayn (two volumes)
Max Frisch
Gorky
Harley Granville Barker
   (two volumes)
Henrik Ibsen (six volumes)
Terry Johnson
Lorca (three volumes)

Marivaux
Mustapha Matura
David Mercer (two volumes)
Arthur Miller
   (five volumes)
Anthony Minghella
Molière
Tom Murphy
   (three volumes)
Musset
Peter Nichols (two volumes)
Clifford Odets
Joe Orton
Louise Page
A. W. Pinero
Luigi Pirandello
Stephen Poliakoff
   (two volumes)
Terence Rattigan
Ntozake Shange
Sophocles (two volumes)
Wole Soyinka
David Storey (two volumes)
August Strindberg
   (three volumes)
J. M. Synge
Ramón del Valle-Inclán
Frank Wedekind
Oscar Wilde

Methuen Student Editions

John Arden	*Serjeant Musgrave's Dance*
Alan Ayckbourn	*Confusions*
Aphra Behn	*The Rover*
Edward Bond	*Lear*
Bertolt Brecht	*The Caucasian Chalk Circle*
	Life of Galileo
	Mother Courage and her Children
Anton Chekhov	*The Cherry Orchard*
Caryl Churchill	*Top Girls*
Shelagh Delaney	*A Taste of Honey*
John Galsworthy	*Strife*
Robert Holman	*Across Oka*
Henrik Ibsen	*A Doll's House*
Charlotte Keatley	*My Mother Said I Never Should*
John Marston	*The Malcontent*
Willy Russell	*Blood Brothers*
August Strindberg	*The Father*
J. M. Synge	*The Playboy of the Western World*
Oscar Wilde	*The Importance of Being Earnest*
Tennessee Williams	*A Streetcar Named Desire*
Timberlake Wertenbaker	*Our Country's Good*